CHARLOTTE BRONTË
A MONOGRAPH

BY

T. WEMYSS REID

First published in 1877

This edition published by Read Books Ltd.
Copyright © 2018 Read Books Ltd.
This book is copyright and may not be
reproduced or copied in any way without
the express permission of the publisher in writing

British Library Cataloguing-in-Publication Data
A catalogue record for this book is available
from the British Library

CONTENTS

INTRODUCTORY	13
THE STORY OF "JANE EYRE."	18
EARLY HISTORY OF THE BRONTËS.	23
THE FAMILY AT HAWORTH.	35
LIFE AS A GOVERNESS.	48
THE TURNING-POINT.	60
AUTHORSHIP AND BEREAVEMENT.	74
"SHIRLEY."	96
LONELINESS AND FAME.	109
"VILLETTE."	124
MARRIAGE AND DEATH.	146
POSTHUMOUS HONOURS.	179
THE BRONTË NOVELS.	193
CONCLUSION.	212

REV. PATRICK BRONTË.

To the Right Honourable
THE LORD HOUGHTON, D.C.L. F.R.S. &c.
THIS MEMORIAL OF A LIFE
WHICH HAS ADDED A NEW GLORY TO THE
LITERARY HISTORY OF YORKSHIRE
IS RESPECTFULLY INSCRIBED BY HIS GRATEFUL
FRIEND
THE AUTHOR.

PREFACE.

I have spoken so freely in the opening chapter of this Monograph of the circumstances under which it has been written, that very little need be said by way of introduction here. This attempt to throw some fresh light upon the character of one of the most remarkable women of our age has not been a task lightly taken up, or hastily performed. The life and genius of Charlotte Brontë had long engaged my attention before I undertook, at the request of the lady to whom I am indebted for most of the original materials I have employed in these pages, the work which I have now completed. In executing that work I have had ample reason to feel and acknowledge my own deficiencies. With the knowledge that I was treading in the footsteps of so consummate a literary artist as Mrs. Gaskell, I have been compelled to refrain from writing not a few of the chapters in Charlotte Brontë's life which are necessary to a complete acquaintance with her character, simply because they had been written so well already. And whilst I necessarily shrink from any appearance of rivalry with Charlotte Brontë's original biographer, I have been additionally oppressed by the feeling that the pen which can do full justice to one of the most moving and noble stories in English literature has not yet been found. But I have been sustained both by the sympathy of many friends, known and unknown, who share my feelings with regard to the Brontës, and by the invaluable assistance rendered to me by those who were intimately acquainted with the household at Haworth Parsonage. Foremost among these must be mentioned Miss Ellen Nussey, the schoolfellow and life-long friend of Charlotte Brontë, who has freely placed at my disposal all the letters and other materials she possessed from which any light could be thrown upon the career of her old companion, and who has in addition aided me with much valuable counsel and advice in the decision of many difficult points. Miss Wooler, who was Charlotte's attached teacher, and who still happily survives in a green old age, has also placed me under obligations by her readiness to supply me with her pupil's letters to herself. Nor must I omit to mention my indebtedness to Lord Houghton for information upon questions which could only be decided by those who met "Currer Bell" during her brief visits to London at a time when she was one of the literary lions of society.

The additions made in this volume to the Monograph as it originally appeared in *Macmillan's Magazine* are numerous and considerable. It should be mentioned that a few of the letters now published (about twenty) were printed some years ago in an American magazine now extinct. The remainder, and by far the larger portion, will be entirely new to readers alike in England and the United States.

Headingley Hill, Leeds,
February, 1877.

THE NEW BRONTË TABLET

To the Memory of the Author of "Jane Eyre."

Beside her sisters lay her down to rest,
By the lone church that stands amid the moors;
And let her grave be wet with moorland showers;
Let moorland larks sing o'er her mouldering breast!
Hers was the keen true spirit, that confest
That she was nurtured in no garden bowers,
Nor taught to deck her brow with cultured flowers,
Nor by the soft and summer wind carest.
Her words came o'er us, as in harvest-tide
Come the swift rain-clouds o'er her native skies,
Scattering the thin sheaves by the heather's side;
So fared it with our tame hypocrisies:
But lo! the clouds are past, and far and wide
The purple ridges glow beneath our eyes.

W. H. CHARLTON.
Hesleyside, 1855.

CHARLOTTE BRONTË

I.

INTRODUCTORY

It is just twenty years since one of the most fascinating and artistic biographies in the English language was given to the world. Mrs. Gaskell's "Life of Charlotte Brontë" no sooner appeared than it took firm possession of the public mind; and it has ever since retained its hold upon all who take an interest in the career of one who has been called, in language which is far less extravagant in reality than in appearance, "the foremost woman of her age." Written with admirable skill, in a style at once powerful and picturesque, and with a sympathy such as only one artist could feel for another, it richly merited the popularity which it gained and has kept. Mrs. Gaskell, however, laboured under one serious disadvantage, which no longer exists in anything like the same degree in which it did twenty years ago. Writing but a few months after Charlotte Brontë had been laid in her grave, and whilst the father to whom she was indebted for so much that was characteristic in her life and genius was still living, Mrs. Gaskell had necessarily to deal with many circumstances which affected living persons too closely to be handled in detail. Even as it was she involved herself in serious embarrassment by some of her allusions to incidents connected more or less nearly with the life of Charlotte Brontë; corrections and retractations were forced upon her, the later editions of the book differed considerably from the first, and at last she was compelled to announce that any further correspondence concerning it must be conducted through her solicitors. Thus she was crippled in her attempt to paint a full-length picture of a remarkable life, and her story was what Mr. Thackeray called it, "necessarily incomplete, though most touching and admirable."

There was, moreover, another matter in which Mrs. Gaskell was at fault. She seems to have set out with the determination that her work should be pitched in a particular key. She had formed her own conception of Charlotte Brontë's character, and with the passion of the true artist and the ability of the practised writer she made everything bend to that conception. The result was that whilst she produced a singularly striking and effective portrait of her heroine, it was not one which was absolutely satisfactory to those who were the oldest and closest friends of Charlotte Brontë. If the truth must be told, the life of the author of "Jane Eyre" was by no means so joyless as the world now believes it to have been. That during the later years in which this wonderful woman produced the works by which she has made her name famous, her career was clouded by sorrow and oppressed by anguish both mental and physical, is perfectly true. That she was made what she was in the furnace of affliction cannot be doubted; but it is not true that she was throughout her whole life the victim of that extreme depression of spirits which afflicted her at rare intervals, and which Mrs. Gaskell has presented to us with so much vividness and emphasis. On the contrary, her letters show that at any rate up to the time of her leaving for Brussels, she was a happy and high-spirited girl, and that even to the very last she had the faculty of overcoming her sorrows by means of that steadfast courage which was her most precious possession, and to which she was so much indebted for her successive victories over trials and disappointments of no ordinary character. Those who imagine that Charlotte Brontë's spirit was in any degree a morbid or melancholy one do her a singular injustice. Intensely reserved in her converse with all save the members of her own household, and the solitary friend to whom she clung with such passionate affection throughout her life, she revealed to these

> The other side, the novel
> Silent silver lights and darks undreamed of,

which were and have remained hidden from the world, but which must be seen by those who would know what Charlotte Brontë really was as a woman. Alas! those who knew her and her sisters well during their brief lives are few in number now. The Brontës who plucked the flower of fame out of the thorny waste in which their lots were cast survive in their books and in Mrs. Gaskell's biography. But the Brontës, the women who lived and suffered thirty years ago, and whose characters were instinct with so rare and lofty a nobility, so keen a sensitiveness, so pure a nobility, are known no longer.

Yet one mode of making acquaintance with them is still open to some among us. From her school-days down to the hour in which she was stretched prostrate in her last sickness, Charlotte Brontë kept up the closest and most confidential intercourse with her one life-long friend. To that friend she addressed letters which may be counted by hundreds, scarcely one of which fails to contain some characteristic touch worthy of the author of "Villette." No one can read this remarkable correspondence without learning the secret of the writer's character; none, as I believe, can read it without feeling that the woman who "stole like a shadow" into the field of English literature in 1847, and in less than eight years after stole as noiselessly away, was truer and nobler even than her works, truer and nobler even than that masterly picture of her life for which we are indebted to Mrs. Gaskell.

These letters lie before me as I write. Here are the faded sheets of 1832, written in the school-girl's hand, filled with the school-girl's extravagant terms of endearment, yet enriched here and there by sentences which are worthy to live—some of which have already, indeed, taken their place in the literature of England; and here is the faint pencil note written to "my own dear Nell" out of the writer's "dreary sick-bed," which was so soon to be the bed of death! Between the first letter and that last sad note what outpourings of the mind of Charlotte Brontë are embodied in this precious pile of cherished manuscript! Over five-and-twenty years of a blameless life this artless record stretches. So far as Charlotte Brontë's history as a woman, and the history of her family are concerned, it is complete for the whole of that period, the only breaks in the story being those which occurred when she and her friend were together. Of her early literary ventures we find little here, for even to her friend she did not dare in the first instance to betray the novel joys which filled her soul when she at last discovered her true vocation, and spoke to a listening world; but of her later life as an author, of her labours from the day when she owned "Jane Eyre" as the child of her brain, there are constant and abundant traces. Here, too, we read all her secret sorrows, her hopes, her fears, her communings with her own heart. Many things there are in this record too sacred to be given to the world. Even now it is with a tender and a reverent hand that one must touch these "noble letters of the dead;" but those who are allowed to see them, to read them and ponder over them, must feel as I do, that the soul of Charlotte Brontë stands revealed in these unpublished pages, and that only here can we see what manner of woman this really was who in the solitude and obscurity of the Yorkshire hill-parsonage built up for herself an imperishable name, enriched the literature of England with treasures of priceless value, and withal led for nearly forty years a life that was made sacred and noble by the self-repression and patient endurance which were its most marked characteristics.

Mrs. Gaskell has done her work so well that the world would scarcely care to listen to a mere repetition of the Brontë story, even though the story-teller were as gifted as the author of "Ruth" herself. But those who have been permitted to gain a new insight into Charlotte Brontë's character, those who are allowed to command materials of which the biographer of 1857 could make no use, may venture to lay a tribute-wreath of their own upon the altar of this great woman's memory—a tribute-wreath woven of flowers culled from her own letters. And it cannot be that the time is yet come when the name or the fame or the touching story of the unique and splendid genius to whom we owe "Jane Eyre," will fall upon the ears of English readers like "a tale of little meaning" or of doubtful interest.

II.

THE STORY OF "JANE EYRE."

In the late autumn of 1847 the reading public of London suddenly found itself called to admire and wonder at a novel which, without preliminary puff of any kind, had been placed in its hands. "'Jane Eyre,' by Currer Bell," became the theme of every tongue, and society exhausted itself in conjectures as to the identity of the author, and the real meaning of the book. It was no ordinary book, and it produced no ordinary sensation. Disfigured here and there by certain crudities of thought and by a clumsiness of expression which betrayed the hand of a novice, it was nevertheless lit up from the first page to the last by the fire of a genius the depth and power of which none but the dullest could deny. The hand of its author seized upon the public mind whether it would or no, and society was led captive, in the main against its will, by one who had little of the prevailing spirit of the age, and who either knew nothing of conventionalism, or despised it with heart and soul. Fierce was the revolt against the influence of this new-comer in the wide arena of letters, who had stolen in, as it were in the night, and taken the citadel by surprise. But for the moment all opposition was beaten down by sheer force of genius, and "Jane Eyre" made her way, compelling recognition, wherever men and women were capable of seeing and admitting a rare and extraordinary intellectual supremacy. "How well I remember," says Mr. Thackeray, "the delight and wonder and pleasure with which I read 'Jane Eyre,' sent to me by an author whose name and sex were then alike unknown to me; and how with my own work pressing upon me, I could not, having taken the volumes up, lay them down until they were read through." It was the same everywhere. Even those who saw nothing to commend in the story, those who revolted against its free employment of great passions and great griefs, and those who were elaborately critical upon its author's ignorance of the ways of polite society, had to confess themselves bound by the spell of the magician. "Jane Eyre" gathered admirers fast; and for every admirer she had a score of readers.

Those who remember that winter of nine-and-twenty years ago know how something like a "Jane Eyre" fever raged among us. The story which had suddenly discovered a glory in uncomeliness, a grandeur in overmastering passion, moulded the fashion of the hour, and "Rochester airs" and "Jane Eyre graces" became the rage. The book, and its fame and influence, travelled beyond the seas with a speed which in those days was marvellous. In sedate New England homes the history of the English governess was read with an avidity which was not surpassed in London itself, and within a few months of the publication of the novel it was famous throughout two continents. No such triumph has been achieved in our time by any other English author; nor can it be said, upon the whole, that many triumphs have been better merited. It happened that this anonymous story, bearing the unmistakable marks of an unpractised hand, was put before the world at the very moment when another great masterpiece of fiction was just beginning to gain the ear of the English public. But at the moment of publication "Jane Eyre" swept past "Vanity Fair" with a marvellous and impetuous speed which left Thackeray's work in the distant background; and its unknown author in a few weeks gained a wider reputation than that which one of the master minds of the century had been engaged for long years in building up.

The reaction from this exaggerated fame, of course, set in, and it was sharp and severe. The blots in the book were easily hit; its author's unfamiliarity with the stage business of the play was evident enough—even to dunces; so it was a simple matter to write smart articles at the expense of a novelist who laid himself open to the whole battery of conventional criticism. In "Jane Eyre" there was much painting of souls in their naked reality; the writer had gauged depths which the plummet of the common story-teller could never have sounded, and conflicting passions were marshalled on the stage with a masterful daring which Shakespeare might have envied; but the costumes, the conventional by-play, the scenery, even the wording of the dialogue, were poor enough in all conscience. The merest playwright or reviewer could have done better in these matters—as the unknown author was soon made to understand. Additional piquancy was given to the attack by the appearance, at the very time when the "Jane Eyre" fever was at its height, of two other novels, written by persons whose sexless names proclaimed them the brothers or the sisters of Currer Bell. Human nature is not so much changed from what it was in 1847 that one need apologise for the readiness with which the reading world in general, and the critical world in particular, adopted the theory that "Wuthering Heights" and "Agnes Grey" were earlier works from the pen which had given them "Jane Eyre." In "Wuthering Heights" some of the faults of the other book were carried to an extreme, and some of its conspicuous merits were distorted and exaggerated until they became positive blemishes; whilst "Agnes Grey" was a feeble and commonplace tale which it was easy to condemn. So the author of "Jane Eyre" was compelled to bear not only her own burden, but that of the two stories which had followed the successful novel; and the reviewers—ignorant of the fact that they were killing three birds at a single shot—rejoiced in the larger scope which was thus afforded to their critical energy.

Here and there, indeed, a manful fight on behalf of Currer Bell was made by writers who knew nothing but the name and the book. "It is soul speaking to soul," cried *Fraser's Magazine* in December, 1847; "it is not a book for prudes," added *Blackwood*, a few months later; "it is not a book for effeminate and tasteless men;

it is for the enjoyment of a feeling heart and critical understanding." But in the main the verdict of the critics was adverse. It was discovered that the story was improper and immoral; it was said to be filled with descriptions of "courtship after the manner of kangaroos," and to be impregnated with a "heathenish doctrine of religion;" whilst there went up a perfect chorus of reprobation directed against its "coarseness of language," "laxity of tone," "horrid taste," and "sheer rudeness and vulgarity." From the book to the author was of course an easy transition. London had been bewildered, and its literary quidnuncs utterly puzzled, when such a story first came forth inscribed with an unknown name. Many had been the rumours eagerly passed from mouth to mouth as to the real identity of Currer Bell. Upon one point there had, indeed, been something like unanimity among the critics, and the story of "Jane Eyre" had been accepted as something more than a romance, as a genuine autobiography in which real and sorrowful experiences were related. Even the most hostile critic of the book had acknowledged that "it contained the story of struggles with such intense suffering and sorrow, as it was sufficient misery to know that any one had conceived, far less passed through." Where then was this wonderful governess to be found? In what obscure hiding-place could the forlorn soul, whose cry of agony had stirred the hearts of readers everywhere, be discovered? We may smile now, with more of sadness than of bitterness, at the base calumnies of the hour, put forth in mere wantonness and levity by a people ever seeking to know some new thing, and to taste some new sensation. The favourite theory of the day—a theory duly elaborated and discussed in the most orthodox and respectable of the reviews—was that Jane Eyre and Becky Sharp were merely different portraits of the same character; and that their original was to be found in the person of a discarded mistress of Mr. Thackeray, who had furnished the great author with a model for the heroine of "Vanity Fair," and had revenged herself upon him by painting him as the Rochester of "Jane Eyre!" It was after dwelling upon this marvellous theory of the authorship of the story that the *Quarterly Review*, with Pecksniffian charity, calmly summed up its conclusions in these memorable words: "If we ascribe the book to a woman at all, we have no alternative but to ascribe it to one who has for some sufficient reason long forfeited the society of her own sex."

The world knows the truth now. It knows that these bitter and shameful words were applied to one of the truest and purest of women; to a woman who from her birth had led a life of self-sacrifice and patient endurance; to a woman whose affections dwelt only in the sacred shelter of her home, or with companions as pure and worthy as herself; to one of those few women who can pour out all their hearts in converse with their friends, happy in the assurance that years hence the stranger into whose hands their frank confessions may pass will find nothing there that is not loyal, true, and blameless. There was wonder among the critics, wonder too in the gay world of London, when the secret was revealed, and men were told that the author of "Jane Eyre" was no passionate light-o'-love who had merely transcribed the sad experiences of her own life; but "an austere little Joan of Arc," pure, gentle, and high-minded, of whom Thackeray himself could say that "a great and holy reverence of right and truth seemed to be with her always." The quidnuncs had searched far and wide for the author of "Jane Eyre;" but we may well doubt whether, when the truth came out at last, they were not more than ever mystified by the discovery that Currer Bell was Charlotte Brontë, the young daughter of a country parson in a remote moorland parish of Yorkshire.

That such a woman should have written such a book was more than a nine days' wonder; and for the key to that which is one of the great marvels and mysteries of English literature we must go to Charlotte Brontë's life itself.

III.

EARLY HISTORY OF THE BRONTËS.

There is a striking passage in Mr. Greg's "Enigmas of Life," in which the influence of external circumstances upon the inner lives of men and women is dwelt upon somewhat minutely, and, by way of example, the connection between religious "conviction" and an imperfect digestion is carefully traced out. That we are the creatures of circumstance can hardly be doubted, nor that our destinies are moulded, just as the coral reefs are built, by the action of innumerable influences, each in itself apparently trivial and insignificant. But the habit which leads men to find a full explanation of the lives of those who have attained exceptional distinction in the circumstances amid which their lot has been cast cannot be said to be a very wholesome or happy one. Few have suffered more cruelly from this trick than the Brontë family. Graphic pictures have been presented to the world of their home among the hills, and of their surroundings in their early years; whilst the public have been asked to believe that some great shadow of gloom rested over their lives from their birth, and that to this fact, and to the influence of the moors, must be attributed, not only the peculiar bent of their genius, but the whole colour and shape of their lives. Those who are thus determined to account for everything that lies out of the range of common experience would do well, before they attempt to analyse the great mystery of genius, to reveal to us the true cause of the superlative excellence of this or that rare *cru*, the secret which gives Johannisberg or Château d'Yquem its glory in the eyes of connoisseurs. Circumstances apparently have little to do with the production of the fragrance and bouquet of these famous wines; for we know that grapes growing close at hand on similar vines and seemingly under precisely similar conditions, warmed by the same sun, refreshed by the same showers, fanned by the same breezes, produce a wine which is comparatively worthless. When the world has expounded this riddle, it will be time enough to deal with that deeper problem of genius on which we are now too apt to lay presumptuous and even violent hands.

The Brontës have suffered grievously from this fashion, inasmuch as their picturesque and striking surroundings have been allowed to obscure our view of the women themselves. We have made a picture of their lives, and have filled in the mere accessories with such pre-Raphaelite minuteness that the distinct individuality of the heroines has been blurred and confused amid the general blaze of vivid colour, the crowd of "telling" points. No individual is to be blamed for this fact. The world, as we have seen, was first introduced to "Currer Bell" and her sisters under romantic circumstances; the lives of those simple, sternly-honest women were enveloped from the moment when the public made their acquaintance in a certain haze of romantic mystery; and when all had passed away, and the time came for the "many-headed beast" to demand the full satisfaction of its curiosity, it would have nothing but the completion of that romance which from the first it had figured in outline for itself.

Who then does not know the salient points of that strange and touching story which tells us how the author of "Jane Eyre" lived and died? Who is not acquainted with that grim parsonage among the hills, where the sisters dwelt amidst such uncongenial and even weird influences; living like recluses in the house of a Protestant pastor; associated with sorrow and suffering, and terrible pictures of degrading vice, during their blameless maidenhood; constructing an ideal world of their own, and dwelling in it heedless of the real world which was in motion all around them? Who has not been amused and interested by those graphic pictures of Yorkshire life in the last century, in which the local flavour is so intense and piquant, and which are hardly the less interesting because they relate to an order of things which had passed away entirely long before the Brontës appeared upon the stage? And who has not been moved by the dark tragedy of Branwell Brontë's life, hinted at rather than explicitly stated, in Mrs. Gaskell's story, but yet standing out in such prominence that those who know no better may be forgiven if they regard it as having been the powerful and all-pervading influence which made the career of the sisters what it was? The true charm of the history of the Brontës, however, does not lie in these things. It is not to be found in the surroundings of their lives, remarkable and romantic as they were, but in the women themselves, and in those characteristics of their hearts and their intellects which were independent of the accidents of condition. Charlotte herself would have been the first to repudiate the notion that there was anything strikingly exceptional in their outward circumstances. With a horror of being considered eccentric that amounted to a passion, she united an almost morbid dread of the notice of strangers. If she could ever have imagined that readers throughout the world would come to associate her name, and still more the names of her idolised sisters, with the ruder features of the Yorkshire character, or with such a domestic tragedy as that amid which her unhappy brother's life terminated, her spirit would have arisen in indignant revolt against that which she would have regarded almost in the light of a personal outrage.

HAWORTH VILLAGE.

And yet if their surroundings at Haworth had comparatively little to do with the development of the genius of the three sisters, it cannot be doubted that two influences which Mrs. Gaskell has rightly made prominent in her book did affect their characters, one in a minor, and the other in a very marked degree. The influence of the moors is to be traced both in their lives and their works; whilst far more distinctly is to be traced the influence of their father. As to the first there is little to be said in addition to that which all know already. There is a railway station now at Haworth, and all the world therefore can get to the place without difficulty or inconvenience. Yet even to-day, when the engine goes, shrieking past it many times between sunrise and sunset, Haworth is not as other places are. A little manufacturing village, sheltered in a nook among the hills and moors which stretch from the heart of Yorkshire into the heart of Lancashire, it bears the vivid impress of its situation. The moors which lie around it for miles on every side are superb during the summer and autumn months. Then Haworth is in its glory; a gray stone hamlet set in the midst of a vast sea of odorous purple, and swept by breezes which bear into its winding street the hum of the bees and the fragrance of the heather. But it is in the drear, leaden days of winter, when the moors are covered with snow, that we see what Haworth really is. Then we know that this is a place apart from the outer world; even the railway seems to have failed to bring it into the midst of that great West Riding which lies close at hand with its busy mills and multitudes; and the dullest therefore can understand that in the days when the railway was not, and Haworth lay quite by itself, neglected and unseen in its upland valley, its people must have been blessed by some at least of those insular peculiarities which distinguished the villagers of Zermatt and Pontresina before the flood of summer tourists had swept into those comparatively remote crannies of the Alps. Nurtured among these lonely moors, and accustomed, as all dwellers on thinly-peopled hillsides are, to study the skies and the weather, as the inhabitants of towns and plains study the faces of men and women, the Brontës unquestionably drew their love of nature, their affection for tempestuous winds and warring clouds, from their residence at Haworth.

But this influence was trivial compared with the hereditary influences of their father's character. Few more remarkable personalities than that of the Rev. Patrick Brontë have obtruded themselves upon the smooth uniformity of modern society. The readers of Mrs. Gaskell's biography know that the incumbent of Haworth was an eccentric man, but the full measure of his eccentricity and waywardness has never yet been revealed to the world. He was an Irishman by birth, but when still a young man he had gone to Yorkshire as a curate, and in Yorkshire he remained to the end of his days. His real name was not Brontë—regarding the origin of which word there was so much unnecessary mystery when his daughter became famous—but Prunty. Born of humble parentage in the parish of Ahaderg, County Down, he was one of a large family, all of whom were said to be remarkable for their physical strength and personal beauty.

Patrick Prunty was the most remarkable member of the family, and his talents were early recognised by Mr. Tighe, the rector of Drumgooland. This gentleman undertook part at least of the cost of his education, which was completed at St. John's College, Cambridge. As to the change of name from Prunty to Brontë, many fantastic stories have been told. Amongst them is one which represents the Brontës as having derived their name from that of the Bronterres, an ancient Irish family with which they were connected. The connection may possibly have existed, but there is no doubt upon one point. The incumbent of Haworth in early life bore the name of Prunty, and it was not until very shortly, before he left Ireland for England that he changed it, at the request of his patron, Mr. Tighe, for the more euphonious appellation of Brontë. He appears to have been a strange compound of good and evil. That he was not without some good is acknowledged by all who knew him. He had kindly feelings towards most people, and he delighted in the stern rectitude which distinguished many of his Yorkshire flock. When his daughter became famous, no one was better pleased at the circumstance than he was. He cut out of every newspaper every scrap which referred to her; he was proud of her achievements, proud of her intellect, and jealous for her reputation. But throughout his whole life there was but one person with whom he had any real sympathy, and that person was himself. Passionate, self-willed, vain, habitually cold and distant in his demeanour towards those of his own household, he exhibited in a marked degree many of the characteristics which Charlotte Brontë afterwards sketched in the portrait of the Mr. Helston of "Shirley." The stranger who encountered him found a scrupulously polite gentleman of the old school, who was garrulous about his past life, and who needed nothing more than the stimulus of a glass of wine to become talkative on the subject of his conquests over the hearts of the ladies of his acquaintance. As you listened to the quaintly-attired old man who chatted on with inexhaustible volubility, you possibly conceived the idea that he was a mere fribble, gay, conceited, harmless; but at odd times a searching glance from the keen, deep-sunk eyes warned you that you also were being weighed in the balance by your companion, and that this assumption of light-hearted vanity was far from revealing the real man to you. Only those who dwelt under the same roof knew him as he really was. Among the many stories told of him by his children, there is one relating to the meek and gentle woman who was his wife, and whose lot it was to submit to persistent coldness and neglect. Somebody had given Mrs. Brontë a very pretty dress, and her husband, who was as proud as he was self-willed, had taken offence at the gift. A word to his wife, who lived in habitual dread of her lordly master, would have secured all he wanted; but in his passionate determination that she should not wear the obnoxious garment, he deliberately cut it to pieces, and presented her with the tattered fragments. Even during his wife's lifetime he formed the habit of taking his meals alone; he constantly carried loaded pistols in his pockets, and when excited he would fire these at the doors of the outhouses, so that the villagers were quite accustomed to the sound of pistol-shots at any hour of the day in their pastor's house. It would be a mistake to suppose that violence was one of the weapons to which Mr. Brontë habitually resorted. However stern and peremptory might be his dealings with his wife (who soon left him to spend the remainder of his life in a dreary widowhood), his general policy was to secure his end by craft rather than by force. A profound belief in his own superior wisdom was conspicuous among his characteristics, and he felt convinced that no one was too clever to be outwitted by his diplomacy. He had also an amazing persistency, which led him to pursue any course on which he had embarked with dogged determination. It happened in later years, when his strength was failing, and when at last he began to see his daughter in her true light, that he quarrelled with her regarding the character of one of their friends. The daughter, always dutiful and respectful, found that any effort to stem the torrent of his bitter and unjust wrath when he spoke of the friend who had offended him, was attended by consequences which were positively dangerous. The veins of his forehead swelled, his eyes glared, his voice shook, and she was fain to submit lest her father's passion should prove fatal to him. But when, wounded beyond endurance by his violence and injustice, she withdrew for a few days from her home, and told her father that she would receive no letters from him in which this friend's name was mentioned, the old man's cunning took the place of passion. He wrote long and affectionate letters to her on general subjects; but accompanying each letter was a little slip of paper, which professed to be a note from Charlotte's dog Flossy to his "much-respected and beloved mistress," in which the dog, declaring that he saw "a good deal of human nature that was hid from those who had the gift of language," was made to repeat the attacks upon the obnoxious person which Mr. Brontë dared no longer make in his own character.

It was to the care of such a father as this, in the midst of the rude and uncongenial society of the lonely manufacturing village, that six motherless children, five daughters and one son, were left in the year 1821. The parson's children were not allowed to associate with their little neighbours in the hamlet; their aunt, who came to the parsonage after their mother's death, had scarcely more sympathy with them than their father himself; their only friend was the rough but kindly servant Tabby, who pitied the bairns without understanding them, and whose acts of graciousness were too often of such a character as to give them more pain than pleasure. So they grew up strange, lonely, old-fashioned children, with absolutely no knowledge of the world outside; so quiet and demure in their habits that, years afterwards, when they invited some of their Sunday scholars up to the parsonage, and wished to amuse them, they found that they had to ask the scholars to teach them how to play—they had never learned. Carefully secluded from the rest of the world, the little Brontë children found out fashions of their own in the way of amusement, and curious fashions they were. Whilst they were still in the nursery, when the oldest of the family, Maria, was barely nine years old, and Charlotte, the third, was just six, they had begun to take a quaint interest in literature and politics. Heaven knows who it was who first told these wonderful pigmies of the great deeds of a Wellington or the crimes of a Bonaparte; but at an age when other children are generally busy with their bricks or their dolls, and when all life's interests are confined for them within the walls of a nursery, these marvellous Brontës were discussing the life of the Great Duke, and maintaining the Tory cause as ardently as the oldest and sturdiest of the village politicians in the neighbouring inn.

There is a touching story of Charlotte at six years old, which gives us some notion of the ideal life led by the forlorn little girl at this time, when, her two elder sisters having been sent to school, she found herself living at home, the eldest of the motherless brood. She had read "The Pilgrim's Progress," and had been fascinated, young as she was, by that wondrous allegory. Everything in it was to her true and real; her little heart had gone forth with Christian on his pilgrimage to the Golden City, her bright young mind had been fired by the Bedford tinker's description of the glories of the Celestial Place; and she made up her mind that she too would escape from the City of Destruction, and gain the haven towards which the weary spirits of every age have turned with eager longing. But where was this glittering city, with its streets of gold, its gates of pearl, its walls of precious stones, its streams of life and throne of light? Poor little girl! The only place which seemed to her to answer Bunyan's description of the celestial town was one which she had heard the servants discussing with enthusiasm in the kitchen, and its name was Bradford! So to Bradford little Charlotte Brontë, escaping from that Haworth Parsonage which she believed to be a doomed spot, set off one day in 1822. Ingenious persons may speculate if they please upon the sore disappointment which awaited her when, like older people, reaching the place which she had imagined to be Heaven, she found that it was only Bradford. But she never even reached her imaginary Golden City. When her tender feet had carried her a mile along the road, she came to a spot where overhanging trees made the highway dark and gloomy; she imagined that she had come to the Valley of the Shadow of Death, and, fearing to go forward, was presently discovered by her nurse cowering by the roadside.

Of the school-days of the Brontës nothing need be said here. Every reader of "Jane Eyre" knows what Charlotte Brontë herself thought of that charitable institution to which she has given so unenviable a notoriety. There she lost her oldest sister, whose fate is described in the tragic tale of Helen Burns; and it was whilst she was at this place that her second sister, Elizabeth, also died. Only one thing need be added to this dismal record of the stay at Cowan Bridge. During the whole time of their sojourn there, the young Brontës scarcely ever knew what it was to be free from the pangs of hunger.

Charlotte was now the head of the little family; the remaining members of which were her brother Branwell and her sisters Emily and Anne. Mrs. Gaskell has given the world a vivid picture of the life which these four survivors from the hardships of Cowan Bridge led between the years 1825 and 1831. They spent those years at Haworth, almost without care or sympathy. Their father saw little in their lot to interest him, nothing to drag him out of his selfish absorption in his own pursuits; their aunt, a permanent invalid, conceived that her duty was accomplished when she had taught them a few lessons and insisted on their doing a certain amount of needlework every day. For the rest they were left to themselves, and thus early they showed the bent of their genius by spending their time in writing novels.

Mrs. Gaskell has given us some idea of the character of these juvenile performances in a series of extracts which sufficiently indicate their rare merit. She has, however, paid exclusive attention to Charlotte's productions. All readers of the Brontë story will remember the account of the play of "The Islanders," and other remarkable specimens, showing with what real vigour and originality Charlotte could handle her pen whilst she was still in the first year of her teens; but those few persons who have seen the whole of the juvenile library of the family bear testimony to the fact that Branwell and Emily were at least as industrious and successful as Charlotte herself. Indeed, even at this early age, the *bizarre* character of Emily's genius was beginning to manifest itself, and her leaning towards weird and supernatural effects was exhibited whilst she composed her first fairy tales within the walls of her nursery. It may be well to bear in mind the frequency with which the critics have charged Charlotte Brontë with exaggerating the precocity of children. What we know of the early days of the Brontës proves that what would have been exaggeration in any other person was in the case of Charlotte nothing but a truthful reproduction of her own experiences.

Only one specimen of these earliest writings of the Brontës can be quoted here: it is that to which I have already referred, the play of "The Islanders:"

June the 31st, 1829.

The play of "The Islanders" was formed in December, 1827, in the following manner. One night, about the time when the cold sleet and stormy fogs of November are succeeded by the snow-storms and high piercing night-winds of confirmed winter, we were all sitting round the warm blazing kitchen fire, having just concluded a quarrel with Tabby concerning the propriety of lighting a candle, from which she came off victorious, no candles having been produced. A long pause succeeded, which was at length broken by Branwell saying, in a lazy manner, "I don't know what to do." This was echoed by Emily and Anne.

Tabby. Wha, ya may go t' bed.
Branwell. I'd rather do anything than that.
Charlotte. Why are you so glum to-night, Tabby? Oh! suppose we had each an island of our own.

Branwell. If we had, I would choose the Island of Man.
Charlotte. And I would choose the Isle of Wight.
Emily. The Isle of Arran for me.
Anne. And mine shall be Guernsey.

We then chose who should be the chief men in our islands. Branwell chose John Bull, Astley Cooper, and Leigh Hunt; Emily, Walter Scott, Mr. Lockhart, Johnny Lockhart; Anne, Michael Sadler, Lord Bentinck, Sir Henry Halford. I chose the Duke of Wellington and two sons, Christopher North and Co., and Mr. Abernethy. Here our conversation was interrupted by the, to us, dismal sound of the clock striking seven, and we were summoned off to bed.

IV.

THE FAMILY AT HAWORTH.

The years have slipped away, and the Brontës are no longer children. They have passed out of that strange condition of premature activity in which their brains were so busy, their lives so much at variance with the lives of others of their age; they have even "finished" their education, according to the foolish phrase of the world, and, having made some acquaintances and a couple of friends at good Miss Wooler's school at Roehead, Charlotte is again at home, young, hopeful, and in her own way merry, waiting with her brother and her sisters till that mystery of life which seems filled with hidden charms to those who still have it all before them shall be revealed.

One bright June morning in 1833, a handsome carriage and pair is standing opposite the Devonshire Arms at Bolton Bridge, the spot loved by all anglers and artists who know anything of the scenery of the Wharfe. In the carriage with some companions is a young girl, whose face, figure, and manner may be conjured up by all who have read "Shirley," for this pleasant, comely Yorkshire maiden, as we see her on this particular morning, is identical with the Caroline Helston who figures in the pages of that novel. Miss N—— is waiting for her quondam schoolfellow and present bosom friend, Charlotte Brontë, who is coming with her brother and sisters to join in an excursion to the enchanted site of Bolton Abbey hard by. Presently, on the steep road which stretches across the moors to Keighley, the sound of wheels is heard, mingled with the merry speech and merrier laughter of fresh young voices. Shall we go forward unseen, and study the approaching travellers whilst they are still upon the road? Their conveyance is no handsome carriage, but a rickety dogcart, unmistakably betraying its neighbourship to the carts and ploughs of some rural farmyard. The horse, freshly taken from the fields, is driven by a youth who, in spite of his countrified dress, is no mere bumpkin. His shock of red hair hangs down in somewhat ragged locks behind his ears, for Branwell Brontë esteems himself a genius and a poet, and, following the fashion of the times, has that abhorrence of the barber's shears which genius is supposed to affect. But the lad's face is a handsome and a striking one, full of Celtic fire and humour, untouched by the slightest shade of care, giving one the impression of somebody altogether hopeful, promising, even brilliant. How gaily he jokes with his three sisters; with what inexhaustible volubility he pours out quotations from his favourite poets, applying them to the lovely scene around him; and with what a mischievous delight, in his superior nerve and mettle, he attempts feats of charioteering which fill the timid heart of the youngest of the party with sudden terrors! Beside him, in a dress of marvellous plainness and ugliness, stamped with the brand "home-made" in characters which none can mistake, is the eldest of the sisters. Charlotte is talking too; there are bright smiles upon her face; she is enjoying everything around her, the splendid morning, the charms of leafy trees and budding roses, and the ever-musical stream; most of all, perhaps, the charm of her brother's society, and the expectation of that coming meeting with her friend, which is so near at hand. Behind sit a pretty little girl, with fine complexion and delicate regular features, whom the stranger would at once pick out as the beauty of the company, and a tall, rather angular figure, clad in a dress exactly resembling Charlotte's. Emily Brontë does not talk so much as the rest of the party, but her wonderful eyes, brilliant and unfathomable as the pool at the foot of a waterfall, but radiant also with a wealth of tenderness and warmth, show how her soul is expanding under the influences of the scene; how quick she is to note the least prominent of the beauties around her, how intense is her enjoyment of the songs of the birds, the brilliancy of the sunshine, the rich scent of the flower-bespangled hedgerows. If she does not, like Charlotte and Anne, meet her brother's ceaseless flood of sparkling words with opposing currents of speech, she utters at times a strange, deep guttural sound which those who know her best interpret as the language of a joy too deep for articulate expression. Gaze at them as they pass you in the quiet road, and acknowledge that, in spite of their rough and even uncouth exteriors, a happier four could hardly be met with in this favourite haunt of pleasure-seekers during a long summer's day.

Suddenly the dogcart rattles noisily into the open space in front of the Devonshire Arms, and the Brontës see the carriage and its occupants. In an instant there is silence; Branwell contrasts his humble equipage with that which already stands at the inn door, and a flush of mortified pride colours his face; the sisters scarcely note this contrast, but to their dismay they see that their friend is not alone, and each draws a long deep breath, and prepares for that fiercest of all the ordeals they know, a meeting with entire strangers. The laughter is stilled; even Branwell's volubility is at an end; the glad light dies out of their eyes, and when they alight and submit to the process of being introduced to Miss N——'s companions, their faces are as dull and commonplace as their dresses. It is no imaginary scene we have been watching. Miss N—— still recalls that painful moment when the merry talk and laughter of her friends were quenched at sight of the company awaiting them, and when throughout a day to which all had looked forward with anticipations of delight, the three Brontës clung to each other or to their friend, scarcely venturing to speak above a whisper, and betraying in every look and word the positive agony which filled their hearts when a stranger approached them. It was this excessive shyness in the company of those who were unfamiliar to them which was the most marked characteristic of the sisters. The weakness was as much physical as moral; and those who suppose that it was accompanied by any morbid depression of spirits, or any lack of vigour and liveliness when the incubus of a stranger's presence was removed, entirely mistake their true character. Unhappily, first impressions are always strongest, and running through the whole of Mrs. Gaskell's story, may be seen the impression produced at her first meeting with Charlotte Brontë by her nervous shrinking and awkwardness in the midst of unknown faces.

It was not thus with those who, brought into the closest of all fellowship with her, the fellowship of school society, knew the secrets of her heart far better than did any who became acquainted with her in after life. To such the real Charlotte Brontë, who knew no timidity in their presence, was a bold, clever, outspoken and impulsive girl; ready to laugh with the merriest, and not even indisposed to join in practical jokes with the rest of her schoolfellows. The picture we get in the "Life" is that of a victim to secret terrors and superstitious fancies. The real Charlotte Brontë, when stories were current as to the presence of a ghost in the upper chambers of the old schoolhouse at Roehead, did not hesitate to go up to these rooms alone and in the darkness of a winter's night, leaving her companions shivering in terror round the fire downstairs. When she had left school, and began that correspondence with Miss N—— which is the great source of our knowledge, not merely of the course of her life, but of the secrets of her heart, it must not be supposed that she wrote always in that serious spirit which pervades most of the letters quoted by Mrs. Gaskell. On the contrary, those who have access to the letters will find that even some of the passages given in the "Life" are allied to sentences showing that the frame of mind in which they were written was very different from that which it appears to have been. The following letter, written from Haworth in the beginning of 1835, is an example:

> Well, here I am as completely separated from you as if a hundred, instead of seventeen, miles intervened between

us. I can neither hear you nor see you nor feel you. You are become a mere thought, an unsubstantial impression on the memory, which, however, is happily incapable of erasure. My journey home was rather melancholy, and would have been very much so but for the presence and conversation of my worthy companion. I found him a very intelligent man. He told me the adventures of his sailor's life, his shipwreck and the hurricane he had witnessed in the West Indies, with a much better flow of language than many of far greater pretensions are masters of. I thought he appeared a little dismayed by the wildness of the country round Haworth, and I imagine he has carried back a pretty report of it.

What do you think of the course politics are taking? I make this inquiry because I now think you have a wholesome interest in the matter; formerly you did not care greatly about it. B——, you see, is triumphant. Wretch! I am a hearty hater, and if there is any one I thoroughly abhor it is that man. But the Opposition is divided. Red-hots and lukewarms; and the Duke (*par excellence the* Duke) and Sir Robert Peel show no signs of insecurity, although they have been twice beat. So "*courage, mon amie!*" Heaven defend the right! as the old Cavaliers used to say before they joined battle. Now, Ellen, laugh heartily at all that rodomontade. But you have brought it on yourself. Don't you remember telling me to write such letters to you as I wrote to Mary? There's a specimen! Hereafter should follow a long disquisition on books; but I'll spare you that.

Those who turn to Mrs. Gaskell's "Life" will find one of the sentences in this letter quoted, but without the burst of laughter over "all that rodomontade" at the end which shows that Charlotte's interest in politics was not unmingled with the happy levity of youth. Still more striking as an illustration of her true character, with its infinite variety of moods, its sudden transitions from grave to gay, is the letter I now quote:

> Last Saturday afternoon, being in one of my sentimental humours, I sat down and wrote to you such a note as I ought to have written to none but M——, who is nearly as mad as myself; to-day, when I glanced it over, it occurred to me that Ellen's calm eye would look at this with scorn, so I determined to concoct some production more fit for the inspection of common sense. I will not tell you all I think and feel about you, Ellen. I will preserve unbroken that reserve which alone enables me to maintain a decent character for judgment; but for that I should long ago have been set down by all who know me as a Frenchified fool. You have been very kind to me of late, and gentle; and you have spared me those little sallies of ridicule which, owing to my miserable and wretched touchiness of character, used formerly to make me wince as if I had been touched with a hot iron; things that nobody else cares for enter into my mind and rankle there like venom. I know these feelings are absurd, and therefore I try to hide them; but they only sting the deeper for concealment, and I'm an idiot. Ellen, I wish I could live with you always, I begin to cling to you more fondly than ever I did. If we had but a cottage and a competency of our own, I do think we might live and love on till death, without being dependent on any third person for happiness.

Mrs. Gaskell has made a very partial and imperfect use of this letter, by quoting merely from the words "You have been very kind to me of late," down to "they only sting the deeper for concealment." Thus it will be seen that an importance is given to an evanescent mood which it was far from meriting, and that lighter side to Charlotte's character which was prominent enough to her nearest and dearest friends is entirely concealed from the outer world. Again, I say, we must not blame Mrs. Gaskell. Such sentences as those which she omitted from the letter I have just given are not only entirely inconsistent with that ideal portrait of "Currer Bell" which the world had formed for itself out of the bare materials in existence during the author's lifetime, but are also utterly at variance with Mrs. Gaskell's personal conception of Charlotte Brontë's character, founded upon her brief acquaintance with her during her years of loneliness and fame.

The quick transitions which marked her moods in converse with her friends may be traced all through her letters to Miss N——. The quotations I have already made show how suddenly on the same page she passes from gaiety to sadness; and so her letters, dealing as they do with an endless variety of topics, reflect only the mood of the writer at the moment that she penned them, and it is only by reading and studying the whole, not by selecting those which reflect a particular phase of her character, that we can complete the portrait we would fain produce.

Here are some extracts from letters which are not to be found in the "Life," and which illustrate what I have said. They were all written between the beginning of 1832 and the end of 1835:

> Tell M—— I hope she will derive benefit from the perusal of Cobbett's lucubrations; but I beg she will on no account burden her memory with passages to be repeated for my edification, lest I should not fully appreciate either her kindness or their merit, since that worthy personage and his principles, whether private or political, are no great favourites of mine.
>
> I am really very much obliged to you—she writes in September, 1832—for your well-filled and *very* interesting letter. It forms a striking contrast to my brief meagre epistles; but I know you will excuse the utter dearth of news visible in them when you consider the situation in which I am placed, quite out of the reach of all intelligence except what I obtain through the medium of the newspapers,

and I believe you would not find much to interest you in a political discussion, or a summary of the accidents of the week.... I am sorry, very sorry, that Miss —— has turned out to be so different from what you thought her; but, my dearest Ellen, you must never expect perfection in this world; and I know your naturally confiding and affectionate disposition has led you to imagine that Miss —— was almost faultless.... I think, dearest Ellen, our friendship is destined to form an exception to the general rule regarding school friendships. At least I know that absence has not in the least abated the sisterly affection which I feel towards you.

Your last letter revealed a state of mind which promised much. As I read it, I could not help wishing that my own feelings more nearly resembled yours; but unhappily all the good thoughts that enter *my* mind evaporate almost before I have had time to ascertain their existence. Every right resolution which I form is so transient, so fragile, and so easily broken, that I sometimes fear I shall never be what I ought.

I write a hasty line to assure you we shall be happy to see you on the day you mention. As you are now acquainted with the neighbourhood and its total want of society, and with our plain, monotonous mode of life, I do not fear so much as I used to do, that you will be disappointed with the dulness and sameness of your visit. One thing, however, will make the daily routine more unvaried than ever. Branwell, who used to enliven us, is to leave us in a few days, and enter the situation of a private tutor in the neighbourhood of U——. How he will like to settle remains yet to be seen. At present he is full of hope and resolution. I, who know his variable nature and his strong turn for active life, dare not be too sanguine. We are as busy as possible in preparing for his departure, and shirt-making and collar-stitching fully occupy our time.

April, 1835.
The election! the election! that cry has rung even among our lonely hills like the blast of a trumpet. How has it been round the populous neighbourhood of B——? Under what banner have your brothers ranged themselves? the Blue or the Yellow? Use your influence with them; entreat them, if it be necessary on your knees, to stand by their country and religion in this day of danger!... Stuart Wortley, the son of the most patriotic patrician Yorkshire owns, must be elected the representative of his native province. Lord Morpeth was at Haworth last week, and I saw him. My opinion of his lordship is recorded in a letter I wrote yesterday to Mary. It is not worth writing over again, so I will not trouble you with it here.

Even these brief extracts will show that Charlotte Brontë's life at this time was not a morbid one. These years between 1832 and 1835 must be counted among the happiest of her life—of all the lives of the little household at Haworth, in fact. The young people were accustomed to their father's coldness and eccentricity, and to their aunt's dainty distaste for all Northern customs and Northern people, themselves included. Shy they were and peculiar, alike in their modes of life and their modes of thought; but there was a wholesome, healthy happiness about all of them that gave promise of peaceful lives hereafter. Some literary efforts of a humble kind brightened their hopes at this time. Charlotte had written some juvenile poems (not now worth reprinting), and she sought the opinion of Southey upon them. The poet laureate gave her a kindly and considerate answer, which did not encourage her to persevere in these efforts; nor was an attempt by Branwell to secure the patronage of Wordsworth for some productions of his own more successful. Had anybody ventured into the wilds of Haworth parish at this new year of 1835, and made acquaintance with the parson's family, it is easy to say upon whom the attention of the stranger would have been riveted. Branwell Brontë, of whom casual mention is made in one of the foregoing letters, was the hope and pride of the little household. All who knew him at this time bear testimony to his remarkable talents, his striking graces. Small in stature like Charlotte herself, he was endowed with a rare personal beauty. But it was in his intellectual gifts that his chief charm was found. Even his father's dull parishioners recognised the fire of genius in the lad; and any one who cares to go to Haworth now and inquire into the story of the Brontës, will find that the most vivid reminiscences, the fondest memories of the older people in the village, centre in this hapless youth. Ambitious and clever, he seemed destined to play a considerable part in the world. His conversational powers were remarkable; he gave promise of more than ordinary ability as an artist, and he had even as a boy written verses of no common power. Among other accomplishments, more curious than useful, of which he could boast, was the ability to write two letters simultaneously. It is but a small trait in the history of this remarkable family, yet it deserves to be noticed, that its least successful member excelled Napoleon himself in one respect. The great conqueror could dictate half-a-dozen letters concurrently to his secretaries. Branwell Brontë could do more than this. With a pen in each hand, he could write two different letters at the same moment.

Charlotte was Branwell's senior by one year. In 1835, when in her nineteenth year, she was by no means the unattractive person she has been represented as being. There is a little caricature sketched by herself lying before me as I write. In it all the more awkward of her physical points are ingeniously exaggerated. The prominent forehead bulges out in an aggressive manner, suggestive of hydrocephalus, the nose, "tip-tilted like the petal of a flower," and the mouth are made unnecessarily large; whilst the little figure is clumsy and ungainly. But though she could never pretend to beauty, she had redeeming features, her eyes, hair, and massive forehead all being attractive points. Emily, who was two years her junior, had, like Charlotte, a bad complexion; but she was tall and well-formed, whilst her eyes were of remarkable beauty. All through her life her temperament was more than merely peculiar. She inherited not a little of her father's eccentricity, untempered by her father's *savoir faire*. Her aversion to strangers has been already mentioned. When the curates, who formed the only society of Haworth, found their way to the parsonage, she avoided them as though they had brought the pestilence in their train. On the rare occasions when she went out into the world, she would sit absolutely silent in the company of those who were unfamiliar to her. So intense was this reserve that even in her own family, where alone she was at ease, something like dread was mingled with the affection felt towards her. On one occasion, whilst Charlotte's friend was visiting the parsonage, Charlotte herself was unable through illness to take any walks with her. To the amazement of the household, Emily volunteered to accompany Miss N—— on a ramble over the moors. They set off together, and the girl threw aside her reserve, and talked with a freedom and vigour which gave evidence of the real strength of her character. Her companion was charmed with her intelligence and geniality. But on returning to the parsonage Charlotte was found awaiting them, and, as soon as she had a chance of doing so, she anxiously put to Miss N—— the question, "How did Emily behave herself?" It was the first time she had ever been known to invite the company of any one outside the narrow limits of the family circle. Her chief delight was to roam on the moors, followed by her dogs, to whom she would whistle in masculine fashion. Her heart, indeed, was given to these dumb creatures of the earth. She never forgave those who ill-treated them, nor trusted those whom they disliked. One is reminded of Shelley's "Sensitive Plant" by some traits of Emily Brontë:

> If the flowers had been her own infants, she
> Could never have nursed them more tenderly;

and, like the lady of the poem, her tenderness and charity could reach even

> ——the poor banished insects, whose intent,
> Although they did ill, was innocent.

One instance of her remarkable personal courage is related in "Shirley," where she herself is sketched under the character of the heroine. It is her adventure with the mad dog which bit her at the door of the parsonage kitchen whilst she was offering it water. The brave girl took an iron from the fire, where it chanced to be heating, and immediately cauterised the wound on her arm, making a broad, deep scar, which was there until the day of her death. Not until many weeks after did she tell her sisters what had happened. Passionately fond of her home among the hills, and of the rough Yorkshire people among whom she had been reared, she sickened and pined away when absent from Haworth. A strange untamed and untamable character was hers; and none but her two sisters ever seem to have appreciated her remarkable merits, or to have recognised the fine though immature genius which shows itself in every line of the weird story of "Wuthering Heights."

Anne, the youngest of the family, had beauty in addition to her other gifts. Intellectually she was greatly inferior to her sisters; but her mildness and sweetness of temperament won the affections of many who were repelled by the harsher exteriors of Charlotte and Emily.

This was the family which lived happily and quietly among the hills during those years when life with its vicissitudes still lay in the distance. Gay their existence could not be called; but their letters show that it was unquestionably peaceful, happy, and wholesome.

THE HOUSE THAT CHARLOTTE VISITED.

V.

LIFE AS A GOVERNESS.

Moved by the hope of lightening the family expenses and enabling Branwell to get a thorough artistic training at the Royal Academy, Charlotte resolved to go out as a governess. Her first "place" was at her old school at Roehead, where she was with her friend, Miss Wooler, and where she was also very near the home of her confidante, Miss N——. Emily went with her for a time, but she soon sickened and pined for the moors, and after a trial of but a few months she returned to Haworth. A great deal of sympathy has been bestowed upon the Brontës in connection with their lives as governesses; nor am I prepared to say that this sympathy is wholly misplaced. Their reserve, their affection for each other, their ignorance of the world, combined to make "the cup of life as it is mixed for the class termed governesses"—to use Charlotte's own phrase—particularly distasteful to them. But it is a mistake to suppose that they were treated with harshness during their governess life, or that Charlotte, at least, felt her trials to be at all unbearable. It was decidedly unpleasant to sacrifice the independence and the family companionship of Haworth for drudgery and loneliness in the household of a stranger; but it was a duty, and as such it was accepted without repining by two, at least, of the sisters. Emily's peculiar temperament made her quite unfitted for life among strangers; she made many attempts to overcome her reserve, but all were unavailing; and after a brief experience in one or two families in different parts of Yorkshire, she returned to Haworth to reside there permanently as her father's housekeeper. There is no need to dwell upon this episode in the lives of the Brontës. They were living among unfamiliar faces, and had little temptation to display themselves in their true characters, but extracts from a few of Charlotte's letters to her friends will show something of the course of her thought at this time. With the exception of a detached sentence or two these letters will be quite new to the readers of Mrs. Gaskell's "Life:"

> I have been waiting for an opportunity of sending a letter to you as you wished; but as no such opportunity offers itself, I have at length determined to write to you by post, fearing that if I delayed any longer you would attribute my tardiness to indifference. I can scarcely realise the distance that lies between us, or the length of time which may elapse before we meet again. Now, Ellen, I have no news to tell you, no changes to communicate. My life since I saw you last has passed away as monotonously and unvaryingly as ever—nothing but teach, teach, teach, from morning till night. The greatest variety I ever have is afforded by a letter from you, a call from the T——s, or by meeting with a pleasant new book. The "Life of Oberlin," and Legh Richmond's "Domestic Portraiture," are the last of this description I have perused. The latter work strongly attracted and strangely fascinated my attention. Beg, borrow, or steal it without delay, and read the "Memoir of Richmond." That short record of a brief and uneventful life I shall never forget. It is beautiful, not on account of the language in which it is written, not on account of the incidents it details, but because of the simple narration it gives of the life and death of a young, talented, sincere Christian. Get the book, Ellen (I wish I had it to give you), read it, and tell me what you think of it. Yesterday I heard that you had been ill since you were in London. I hope you are better now. Are you any happier than you were? Try to reconcile your mind to circumstances, and exert the quiet fortitude of which I know you are not destitute.

Your absence leaves a sort of vacancy in my feelings which nothing has as yet offered of sufficient interest to supply. I do not forget ten o'clock. I remember it every night, and if a sincere petition for your welfare will do you any good you will be benefited. I know the Bible says: "The prayer of the *righteous* availeth much," and I am *not righteous*. Nevertheless I believe God despises no application that is uttered in sincerity. My own dear E——, good-bye. I can write no more, for I am called to a less pleasant avocation.

Dewsbury Moor, Oct. 2, 1836.

I should have written to you a week ago, but my time has of late been so wholly taken up that till now I have really not had an opportunity of answering your last letter. I assure you I feel the kindness of so early a reply to my tardy correspondence. It gave me a sting of self-reproach.... My sister Emily is gone into a situation as teacher in a large school of near forty pupils, near Halifax. I have had one letter from her since her departure. It gives an appalling account of her duties. Hard labour from six in the morning till near eleven at night, with only one half-hour of exercise between. This is slavery. I fear she will never stand it. It gives me sincere pleasure, my dear Ellen, to learn that you have at last found a few associates of congenial minds. I cannot conceive a life more dreary than that passed amidst sights, sounds, and companions all alien to the nature within us. From the tenor of your letters it seems that your mind remains fixed as it ever was, in no wise dazzled by novelty or warped by evil example. I am thankful for it. I could not help smiling at the paragraphs which related to ——. There was in them a touch of the genuine unworldly simplicity which forms part of your character. Ellen, depend upon it, all people have their dark side. Though some possess the power of throwing a fair veil over the defects, close acquaintance slowly removes the screen, and one by one the blots appear; till at last we see the pattern of perfection all slurred over with stains which even affection cannot efface.

The affectionate commendations of her friend are constantly accompanied by references of a very different character to herself.

If I like people—she says in one of her letters—it is my nature to tell them so, and I am not afraid of offering incense to your vanity. It is from religion that you derive your chief charm, and may its influence always preserve you as pure, as unassuming, and as benevolent in thought and deed as you are now. What am I compared to you? I feel my own utter worthlessness when I make the comparison. I'm a very coarse, commonplace wretch! I have some qualities that make me very miserable, some feelings that you can have no participation in—that few, very few people in the world can at all understand. I don't pride myself on these peculiarities. I strive to conceal and suppress them as much as I can, but they burst out sometimes, and then those who see the explosion despise me, and I hate myself for days afterwards.

All my notes to you, Ellen, are written in a hurry. I am now snatching an opportunity. Mr. J—— is here; by his means it will be transmitted to Miss E——, by her means to X——, by his means to you. I do not blame you for not coming to see me. I am sure you have been prevented by sufficient reasons; but I do long to see you, and I hope I shall be gratified momentarily, at least, ere long. Next Friday, if all be well, I shall go to G——. On Sunday I hope I shall at least catch a glimpse of you. Week after week I have lived on the expectation of your coming. Week after week I have been disappointed. I have not regretted what I said in my last note to you. The confession was wrung from me by sympathy and kindness, such as I can never be sufficiently thankful for. I feel in a strange state of mind; still gloomy, but not despairing. I keep trying to do right, checking wrong feelings; repressing wrong thoughts—but still, every instant I find myself going astray. I have a constant tendency to scorn people who are far better than I am. A horror at the idea of becoming one of a certain set—a dread lest if I made the slightest profession I should sink at once into Phariseeism, merge wholly in the ranks of the self-righteous. In writing at this moment I feel an irksome disgust at the idea of using a single phrase that sounds like religious cant. I abhor myself; I despise myself. If the doctrine of Calvin be true, I am already an outcast. You cannot imagine how hard, rebellious, and intractable all my feelings are. When I begin to study on the subject I almost grow blasphemous, atheistical in my sentiments. Don't desert me—don't be horrified at me. You know what I am. I wish I could see you, my darling. I have lavished the warmest affections of a very hot, tenacious heart upon you. If you grow cold it is over.

You will excuse a very brief and meagre answer to your kind note when I tell you that at the moment it reached me, and that just now whilst I am scribbling a reply, the whole house is in the bustle of packing and preparation, for on this day we all *go home*. Your palliation of my defects is kind and charitable, but I dare not trust its truth. Few would regard them with so lenient an eye as you do. Your consolatory admonitions are kind, Ellen; and when I can read them over in quietness and alone, I trust I shall derive comfort from them. But just now, in the unsettled, excited state of mind which I now feel,

I cannot enter into the pure scriptural spirit which they breathe. It would be wrong of me to continue the subject. My thoughts are distracted and absorbed by other ideas. You do not mention your visit to Haworth. Have you spoken of it to the family? Have they agreed to let you come? But I will write when I get home. Ever since last Friday I have been as busy as I could be in finishing up the half-year's lessons, which concluded with a terrible fog in geographical problems (think of explaining that to Misses —— and ——!), and subsequently in mending Miss ——'s clothes. Miss —— is calling me: something about my *protégée's* nightcap. Good-bye. We shall meet again ere many days, I trust.

Here it will be seen that the religious struggle was renewed. The woman who was afterwards to be accused of "heathenism" was going through tortures such as Cowper knew in his darkest hours, and, like him, was acquiring faith, humility, and resignation in the midst of the conflict. But such letters as this are only episodical; in general she writes cheerfully, sometimes even merrily.

THE ROE HEAD SCHOOL.

What would the *Quarterly* reviewer and the other charitable people, who openly declared their conviction that the author of "Jane Eyre" was an improper person, who had written an improper book, have said had they been told that she had written the following letter on the subject of her first offer of marriage—written it, too, at the time when she was a governess, and in spite of the fact that the offer opened up to her a way of escape from all anxiety as to her future life?

You ask me whether I have received a letter from T——. I have about a week since. The contents I confess did a little surprise me; but I kept them to myself, and unless you had questioned me on the subject I would never have adverted to it. T—— says he is comfortably settled at ——, and that his health is much improved. He then intimates that in due time he will want a wife, and frankly asks me to be that wife. Altogether the letter is written without cant or flattery, and in common-sense style which does credit to his judgment. Now there were in this proposal some things that might have proved a strong temptation. I thought if I were to marry so —— could live with me, and how happy I should be. But again I asked myself two questions: Do I love T—— as much as a woman ought to love her husband? Am I the person best qualified to make him happy? Alas! my conscience answered "No" to both these questions. I felt that though I esteemed T——, though I had a kindly leaning towards him, because he is an amiable, well-disposed man, yet I had not and never could have that intense attachment which would make me willing to die for him—and if ever I marry it must be in that light of adoration that I will regard my husband. Ten to one I shall never have the chance again; but *n'importe*. Moreover, I was aware he knew so little of me he could hardly be conscious to whom he was writing. Why, it would startle him to see me in my natural home character. He would think I was a wild, romantic enthusiast indeed. I could not sit all day long making a grave face before my husband. I would laugh and satirise, and say whatever came into my head first; and if he were a clever man and loved me, the whole world weighed in the balance against his smallest wish would be light as air. Could I, knowing my mind to be such as that, conscientiously say that I would take a grave, quiet young man like T——? No; it would have been deceiving him, and deception of that sort is beneath me. So I wrote a long letter back in which I expressed my refusal as gently as I could, and also candidly avowed my reasons for that refusal. I described to him, too, the sort of character I thought would suit him for a wife.

The girl who could thus calmly decline a more than merely "eligible" offer, and thus honestly state her reasons for doing so to the friend she trusted, was strangely different from the author of "Jane Eyre" pictured by the critics and the public. Perhaps the full cost of the refusal related in the foregoing letter is only made clear when it is brought into contrast with such a confession as the following, made very soon afterwards:

> I am miserable when I allow myself to dwell on the necessity of spending my life as a governess. The chief requisite for that station seems to me to be the power of taking things easily when they come, and of making oneself comfortable and at home wherever one may chance to be—qualities in which all our family are singularly deficient. I know I cannot live with a person like Mrs. ——; but I hope all women are not like her, and my motto is "Try again."

How thoroughly at all times she could sympathise alike with the joys and sorrows of others, is proved by many letters extending over the whole period of her life. The following is neither the earliest nor the most characteristic of those utterances of a tender and heartfelt sympathy with her special friend, which are to be found in her correspondence, but as Mrs. Gaskell has not made use of it, I may quote it here:

1838.

> We were at breakfast when your note reached me, and I consequently write in great hurry. Your trials seem to thicken. I trust God will either remove them or give you strength to bear them. If I could but come to you and offer you all the little assistance either my head or hands

could afford! But that is impossible. I scarcely dare offer to comfort you about —— lest my consolation should seem like mockery. I know that in cases of sickness strangers cannot measure what relations feel. One thing, however, I need not remind *you* of. You will have repeated it over and over to yourself before now: God does all for the best; and even should the worst happen, and Death seem finally to destroy hope, remember that this will be but a practical test of the strong faith and calm devotion which have marked you a Christian so long. I would hope, however, that the time for this test is not yet come, that your brother may recover, and all be well. It grieves me to hear that your own health is so indifferent. Once more I wish I were with you to lighten at least by sympathy the burden that seems so unsparingly laid upon you. Let me thank you for remembering me in the midst of such hurry and affliction. We are all apt to grow selfish in distress. This, so far as I have found, is not your case. *When* shall I see you again? The uncertainty in which the answer to that question must be involved gives me a bitter feeling. Through all changes, through all chances, I trust I shall love you as I do now. We can pray for each other and think of each other. Distance is no bar to recollection. You have promised to write to me, and I do not doubt that you will keep your word. Give my love to M—— and your mother. Take with you my blessing and affection, and all the warmest wishes of a warm heart for your welfare.

From one of her situations as governess in a private family (she had long since left the kind shelter of Miss Wooler's house) she writes in 1841 a series of letters showing how little she relished the "cup of life as it is mixed for the class termed governesses."

It is twelve o'clock at night; but I must just write you a word before I go to bed. If you think I'm going to refuse your invitation, or if you sent it me with that idea, you're mistaken. As soon as I had read your shabby little note, I gathered up my spirits directly, walked on the impulse of the moment into Mrs. ——'s presence, popped the question, and for two minutes received no answer. "Will she refuse me when I work so hard for her?" thought I. "Ye—e—es," drawled madam in a reluctant, cold tone. "Thank you, madam!" said I with extreme cordiality, and was marching from the room when she recalled me with "You'd better go on Saturday afternoon, then, when the children have holiday, and if you return in time for them to have all their lessons on Monday morning, I don't see that much will be lost." You *are* a genuine Turk, thought I; but again I assented, and so the bargain was struck. Saturday after next, then, is the day appointed. I'll come, God knows, with a thankful and joyful heart, glad of a day's reprieve from labour. If you don't send the gig I'll walk. I am coming to taste the pleasure of liberty; a bit of pleasant congenial talk, and a sight of two or three faces I like. God bless you! I want to see you again. Huzza for Saturday afternoon after next! Good-night, my lass!

During the last three weeks that hideous operation called "a thorough clean" has been going on in the house. It is now nearly completed, for which I thank my stars, as during its progress I have fulfilled the double character of nurse and governess, while the nurse has been transmuted into cook and housemaid. That nurse, by-the-bye, is the prettiest lass you ever saw.... I was beginning to think Mrs. —— a good sort of body in spite of her bouncing and toasting, her bad grammar and worse orthography; but I have had experience of one little trait in her character which condemns her a long way with me. After treating a person on the most familiar terms of equality for a long time, if any little thing goes wrong, she does not scruple to give way to anger in a very coarse, unladylike manner, though in justice no blame could be attached where she ascribed it all. I think passion is the true test of vulgarity or refinement. This place looks exquisitely beautiful just now. The grounds are certainly lovely, and all as green as an emerald. I wish you would just come and look at it.

VI.

THE TURNING-POINT.

The "storm and stress" period of Charlotte Brontë's life was not what the world believes it to have been. Like the rest of our race, she had to fight her own battle in the wilderness, not with one devil, but with many; and it was this sharp contest with the temptations which crowd the threshold of an opening life which made her what she was. The world believes that it was under the parsonage roof that the author of "Jane Eyre" gathered up the precious experiences which were afterwards turned to such good account. Mrs. Gaskell, who was carried away by her honest womanly horror of hardened vice, gives us to understand that the tragic turning-point in the history of the sisters was connected with the disgrace and ruin of their brother. We are even asked to believe that but for the folly of a single woman, whom it is probable that Charlotte never saw, "Currer Bell" would never have taken up her pen, and no halo of glory would have settled on the scarred and rugged brows of prosaic Haworth.

It is not so. There may be disappointment among those who have been nurtured on the traditions of the Brontë romance when they find that the reality is different from what they supposed it to be; some shallow judges may even assume that Charlotte herself loses in moral stature when it is shown that it was not her horror at her brother's fall which drove her to find relief in literary speech. But the truth must be told; and for my part I see nothing in that truth which affects, even in an infinitesimal degree, the fame and the honour of the woman of whom I write.

It was Charlotte's visit to Brussels, then, first as pupil and afterwards as teacher in the school of Madame Héger, which was the turning-point in her life, which changed its currents, and gave to it a new purpose and a new meaning. Up to the moment of that visit she had been the simple, kindly, truthful Yorkshire girl, endowed with strange faculties, carried away at times by burning impulses, moved often by emotions the nature of which she could not fathom, but always hemmed in by her narrow experiences, her limited knowledge of life and the world. Until she went to Belgium, her sorest troubles had been associated with her dislike to the society of strangers, her heaviest burden had been the necessity under which she lay of tasting that "cup of life as it is mixed for governesses" which she detested so heartily. Under the belief that they could qualify themselves to keep a school of their own if they had once mastered the delicacies of the French and German languages, she and Emily set off for this sojourn in Brussels.

One may be forgiven for speculating as to her future lot had she accepted the offer of marriage she received in her early governess days, and settled down as the faithful wife of a sober English gentleman. In that case "Shirley" perhaps might have been written, but "Jane Eyre" and "Villette" never. She learnt much during her two years' sojourn in the Belgian capital; but the greatest of all the lessons she mastered whilst there was that self-knowledge the taste of which is so bitter to the mouth, though so wholesome to the life. Mrs. Gaskell has made such ample use of the letters she penned during the long months which she spent as an exile from England, that there is comparatively little left to cull from them. Everybody knows the outward circumstances of her story at this time. For a brief period she had the company of Emily; and the two sisters, working together with the unremitting zeal of those who have learned that time is money, were happy and hopeful, enjoying the novel sights of the gay foreign capital, gathering fresh experiences every day, and looking forward to the moment when they would return to familiar Haworth, and realise the dream of their lives by opening a school of their own within the walls of the parsonage. But then Emily left, and Charlotte, after a brief holiday at home, returned alone. Years after, writing to her friend, she speaks of her return in these words: "I returned to Brussels after aunt's death against my conscience, prompted by what then seemed an irresistible impulse. I was punished for my selfish folly by a total withdrawal for more than two years of happiness and peace of mind." Why did she thus go back "against her conscience?" Her friends declared that her future husband dwelt somewhere within sound of the chimes of St. Gudule, and that she insisted upon returning to Brussels because she was about to be married there. We know now how different was the reality. The husband who awaited her was even then about to begin his long apprenticeship of love at Haworth. Yet none the less had her spirit, if not her heart, been captured and held captive in the Belgian city. It is not in her letters that we find the truth regarding her life at this time. The truth indeed is there, but not all the truth. "In catalepsy and dread trance," says Lucy Snowe, "I studiously held the quick of my nature.... It is on the surface only the common gaze will fall." The secrets of her inner life could not be trusted to paper, even though the lines were intended for no eyes but those of her friend and confidante. There are some things, as we know well, that the heart hides as by instinct, and which even frank and open natures only reveal under compulsion. Writing to her friend from Brussels in October, 1843, she says: "I have much to say, Ellen; many little odd things, queer and puzzling enough, which I do not like to trust to a letter, but which one day, perhaps, or rather one evening, if ever we should find ourselves again by the fireside at Haworth, or at B——, with our feet on the fender, curling our hair, I may communicate to you." One of the hardest features of the last year she spent at Brussels was the necessity she was under of locking all the deepest emotions of her life within her own breast, of preserving the calm and even cold exterior, which should tell nothing to the common gaze, above the troubled, fevered heart that beat within.

When do you think I shall see you?—she cries to her friend within a few days of her final return to Haworth—I have, of course, much to tell you, and I dare say you have much also to tell me—things which we should neither of us wish to commit to paper.... I do not know whether you feel as I do, but there are times now when it appears to me as if all my ideas and feelings, except a few friendships and affections, are changed from what they used to be. Something in me which used to be enthusiasm is tamed down and broken. I have fewer illusions. What I wish for now is active exertion—a stake in life. Haworth seems such a lonely, quiet spot, buried away from the world. I no longer regard myself as young; indeed, I shall soon be twenty-eight, and it seems as if I ought to be working and braving the rough realities of the world, as other people do. It is, however, my duty to restrain this feeling at present, and I will endeavour to do so.

Yes; she was "disillusioned" now, and she had brought back from Brussels a heart which could never be quite so light, a spirit which could never again soar so buoyantly, as in those earlier years when the tree of knowledge was still untasted, and the mystery of life still unrevealed. This stay in Belgium was, as I have said, the turning-point in Charlotte Brontë's career, and its true history and meaning is to be found, not in her "Life" and letters, but in "Villette," the master-work of her mind, and the revelation of the most vivid passages in her own heart's history. "I said I disliked Lucy Snowe," is a remark which Mrs. Gaskell innocently repeats in her memoir of Charlotte Brontë. One need not be surprised at it. Lucy Snowe was never meant to be liked—by everybody; but none the less is Lucy Snowe the truest picture we possess of the real Charlotte Brontë; whilst not a few of the fortunes which befell this strange heroine are literal transcripts from the life of her creator. One little incident in "Villette"—Lucy's impulsive visit to a Roman Catholic confessor—is taken direct from Charlotte's own experience. During one of the long lonely holidays in the foreign school, when her mind was restless and disturbed, her heart heavy, her nerves jarred and jangled, she fled from the great empty schoolrooms to seek peace in the street; and she found, not peace perhaps, but sympathy at least, in the counsels of a priest, seated at the Confessional in a church into which she wandered, who took pity on the little heretic, and soothed her troubled spirit without attempting to enmesh it in the folds of Romanism. It was from experiences such as these, with a chastened heart and a nature tamed down, though by no means broken, that she returned to familiar Haworth, to face "the rough realities of the world."

Rough, indeed, those realities were in her case. Her brother, once the hope of the family, had now become its burden and its curse; and from that moment he was to be the prodigal for whom no fatted calf would ever be killed. Her father was fast losing his eyesight; she and her sisters were getting on in life, and "something must be done." Charlotte had returned home, but her heart was still in Brussels, and the wings of her spirit began to beat impatiently against the cage in which she found herself imprisoned. It was only the old story. She had gone out into the world, had tasted strange joys, and drunk deep of waters the very bitterness of which seemed to endear them to her. Returning to Haworth she went back a new woman, with tastes and hopes which it was hard to reconcile with the monotony of life in the parsonage which had once satisfied her completely.

"If I *could* leave home I should not be at Haworth," she says soon after her return. "I know life is passing away, and I am doing nothing, earning nothing; a very bitter knowledge it is at moments, but I see no way out of the mist." And then, almost for the first time in her life, something like a cry of despair goes up from her lips: "Probably, when I am free to leave home, I shall neither be able to find place nor employment. Perhaps, too, I shall be quite past the prime of life, my faculties will be wasted, and my few acquirements in a great measure forgotten. These ideas sting me keenly sometimes; but whenever I consult my conscience, it affirms that I am doing right in staying at home, and bitter are its upbraidings when I yield to an eager desire for release."

But this outburst of personal feeling was exceptional, and was uttered in one ear only. Within the walls of her home Charlotte again became the house-mother, busying herself with homely cares, and ever watching for some opportunity of carrying her plan of school-keeping into execution. Nor did she allow either the troubles at home, or that weight at her own heart which she bore in secrecy, to render her spirit morbid and melancholy. Not a few who have read Mrs. Gaskell's work labour under the belief that this was the effect that Charlotte Brontë's trials had upon her. As a matter of fact, however, she was far too strong, brave, cheerful—one had almost said manly—to give way to any such selfish repinings. She never was one of those sickly souls who go about "glooming over the woes of existence, and how unworthy God's universe is to have so distinguished a resident." Even when her own sorrows were deepest, and her lot seemed hardest, she found a lively pleasure in discussing the characters and lots of others, and expended as much pains and time in analysing the inner lives of her friends as our sham Byrons are wont to expend upon the study of their own feelings and emotions. Indeed, of that self-pity which is so common a characteristic of the young, no trace is to be found in her correspondence. Let the following letter, hitherto unpublished, written at the very time when the household clouds were blackest, speak for her freedom from morbid self-consciousness, as well as for her hearty interest in the well-being of those around her:

> You are a very good girl indeed to send me such a long and interesting letter. In all that account of the young lady and gentleman in the railway carriage I recognise your faculty for observation, which is a rarer gift than you imagine. You ought to be thankful for it. I never

yet met with an individual devoid of observation whose conversation was interesting, nor with one possessed of that power in whose society I could not manage to pass a pleasant hour. I was amused with your allusions to individuals at ——. I have little doubt of the truth of the report you mention about Mr. Z—— paying assiduous attention to ——. Whether it will ever come to a match is another thing. *Money* would decide that point, as it does most others of a similar nature. You are perfectly right in saying that Mr. Z—— is more influenced by opinion than he himself suspects. I saw his lordship in a new light last time I was at ——. Sometimes I could scarcely believe my ears when I heard the stress he laid on wealth, appearance, family, and all those advantages which are the idols of the world. His conversation on marriage (and he talked much about it) differed in no degree from that of any hackneyed fortune-hunter, except that with his own peculiar and native audacity he avowed views and principles which more timid individuals conceal. Of course I raised no argument against anything he said. I listened, and laughed inwardly to think how indignant I should have been eight years since if anyone had accused Z—— of being a worshipper of Mammon and of Interest. Indeed, I still believe that the Z—— of ten years ago is not the Z—— of to-day. The world, with its hardness and selfishness, has utterly changed him. He thinks himself grown wiser than the wisest. In a worldly sense he is wise. His feelings have gone through a process of petrifaction which will prevent them from ever warring against his interest; but Ichabod! all glory of principle, and much elevation of character are gone! I learnt another thing. Fear the smooth side of Z——'s tongue more than the rough side. He has the art of paying peppery little compliments, which he seems to bring out with a sort of difficulty, as if he were not used to that kind of thing, and did it rather against his will than otherwise. These compliments you feel disposed to value on account of their seeming rarity. Fudge! They are at any one's disposal, and are confessedly hollow blarney.

Still more significant, however, is the following letter, showing so kindly and careful an interest in the welfare of the friend to whom it is addressed, even whilst it bears the bitter tidings of a great household sorrow:

July 31, 1845.

I was glad to get your little packet. It was quite a treasure of interest to me. I think the intelligence about G—— is cheering. I have read the lines to Miss ——. They are expressive of the affectionate feelings of his nature, and are poetical, insomuch as they are true. Faults in expression, rhythm, metre, were of course to be expected. All you say about Mr. —— amused me much. Still, I cannot put out of my mind one fear, viz. that you should think too much about him. Faulty as he is, and as you know him to be, he has still certain qualities which might create an interest in your mind before you were aware. He has the art of impressing ladies by something involuntary in his look and manner, exciting in them the notion that he cares for them, while his words and actions are all careless, inattentive, and quite uncompromising for himself. It is only men who have seen much of life and of the world, and who are become in a measure indifferent to female attractions, that possess this art. So be on your guard. These are not pleasant or flattering words, but they are the words of one who has known you long enough to be indifferent about being temporarily disagreeable, provided she can be permanently useful.

I got home very well. There was a gentleman in the

railroad carriage whom I recognised by his features immediately as a foreigner and a Frenchman. So sure was I of it that I ventured to say to him, "*Monsieur est français, n'est-ce pas?*" He gave a start of surprise, and answered immediately in his own tongue. He appeared still more astonished and even puzzled when, after a few minutes' further conversation, I inquired if he had not passed the greater part of his life in Germany. He said the surmise was correct. I guessed it from his speaking French with the German accent.

It was ten o'clock at night when I got home. I found Branwell ill. He is so very often, owing to his own fault. I was not therefore shocked at first. But when Anne informed me of the immediate cause of his present illness I was very greatly shocked. He had last Thursday received a note from Mr. —— sternly dismissing him..... We have had sad work with him since. He thought of nothing but stunning or drowning his distressed mind. No one in the house could have rest, and at last we have been obliged to send him from home for a week with someone to look after him. He has written to me this morning, and expresses some sense of contrition for his frantic folly. He promises amendment on his return, but so long as he remains at home I scarce dare hope for peace in the house. We must all, I fear, prepare for a season of distress and disquietude. I cannot now ask Miss —— or anyone else.

The gloom in the household deepened; but Charlotte was still strong enough and brave enough to meet the world, to retain her accustomed interest in her friends, and to discuss as of yore the characters and lives of those around her. Curious are the glimpses one gets of her circle of acquaintances at this time. Little did many of those with whom she was brought in contact think of the keen eyes which were gazing out at them from under the prominent forehead of the parson's daughter. Yet not the least interesting feature of her correspondence is the evidence it affords that she was gradually gaining that knowledge of character which was afterwards to be lavished upon her books. A string of extracts from letters hitherto unpublished will suffice to show how the current of her life and thoughts ran in those days of domestic darkness, whilst the dawn of her fame was still hidden in the blackest hour of the night:

> I have just read M——'s letters. They are very interesting, and show the original and vigorous cast of her mind. There is but one thing I could wish otherwise in them, and that is a certain tendency to flightiness. It is not safe, it is not wise; and will often cause her to be misconstrued. Perhaps *flightiness* is not the right word; but it is a devil-may-care tone, which I do not like when it proceeds from under a hat, and still less from under a bonnet.
>
> I return you Miss ——'s notes with thanks. I always like to read them. They appear to me so true an index of an amiable mind, and one not too conscious of its own worth. Beware of awakening in her this consciousness by undue praise. It is a privilege of simple-hearted, sensible, but not brilliant people that they can *be* and *do* good without comparing their own thoughts and actions too closely with those of other people, and thence drawing strong food for self-appreciation. Talented people almost always know full well the excellence that is in them.... You ask me if we are more comfortable. I wish I could say anything favourable; but how can we be more comfortable so long as Branwell stays at home and degenerates instead of improving? It has been lately intimated to him that he would be received again on the same railroad where he was formerly stationed if he would behave more steadily, but he refuses to make an effort. He will not work, and at home he is a drain on every resource, an impediment to

all happiness. But there's no use in complaining.

   I thank you again for your last letter, which I found as full or fuller of interest than either of the preceding ones—it is just written as I wish you to write to me—not a detail too much. A correspondence of that sort is the next best thing to actual conversation, though it must be allowed that between the two there is a wide gulf still. I imagine your face, voice, presence very plainly when I read your letters. Still imagination is not reality, and when I return them to their envelope and put them by in my desk I feel the difference sensibly enough. My curiosity is a little piqued about that countess you mention. What is her name? you have not yet given it. I cannot decide from what you say whether she is really clever or only eccentric. The two sometimes go together, but are often seen apart. I generally feel inclined to fight very shy of eccentricity, and have no small horror of being thought eccentric myself, by which observation I don't mean to insinuate that I class myself under the head clever. God knows a more consummate ass in sundry important points has seldom browsed the green herb of His bounties than I. O Lord, Nell, I'm in danger sometimes of falling into self-weariness. I used to say and to think in former times that X—— would certainly be married. I am not so sanguine on that point now. It will never suit her to accept a husband she cannot love, or at least respect, and it appears there are many chances against her meeting with such a one under favourable circumstances; besides, from all I can hear and see, money seems to be regarded as almost the Alpha and Omega of requisites in a wife. Well, if she is destined to be an old maid I don't think she will be a repining one. I think she will find resources in her own mind and disposition which will help her to get on. As to society, I don't understand much about it, but from the few glimpses I have had of its machinery it seems to me to be a very strange, complicated affair indeed, wherein nature is turned upside down. Your well-bred people appear to me, figuratively speaking, to walk on their heads, to see everything the wrong way up—a lie is with them truth, truth a lie, eternal and tedious botheration is their notion of happiness, sensible pursuits their *ennui*. But this may be only the view ignorance takes of what it cannot understand. I refrain from judging them, therefore, but if I were called upon to *swop*—you know the word, I suppose—to swop tastes and ideas and feelings with ——, for instance, I should prefer walking into a good Yorkshire kitchen fire and concluding the bargain at once by an act of voluntary combustion.

I shall scribble you a short note about nothing, just to have a pretext for screwing a letter out of you in return. I was sorry you did not go to W——, firstly, because you lost the pleasure of observation and enjoyment; and secondly, because I lost the second-hand indulgence of hearing your account of what you had seen. I laughed at the candour with which you give your reason for wishing to be there. Thou hast an honest soul as ever animated human carcase, and a clean one, for it is not ashamed of showing its inmost recesses: only be careful with whom you are frank. Some would not rightly appreciate the value of your frankness, and never cast pearls before swine. You are quite right in wishing to look well in the eyes of those whom you desire to please. It is natural to desire to appear to advantage (*honest* not *false* advantage of course) before people we respect. Long may the power and the inclination to do so be spared you; long may you look young and handsome enough to dress in white; and long may you have a right to feel the consciousness that you look agreeable. I know you have too much judgment to let an over-dose of vanity spoil the blessing and turn it into a misfortune. After all though, age will come on, and it is well you have something better than a nice face for friends to turn to when that is changed. I hope this excessively cold weather has not harmed you or *yours* much. It has nipped me severely—taken away my appetite for a while, and given me toothache; in short put me in the ailing condition in which I have more than once had the honour of making myself such a nuisance both at B—— and ——. The consequence is that at this present speaking I look almost old enough to be your mother—gray, sunk, and withered. To-day, however, it is milder, and I hope soon to feel better; indeed, I am not *ill* now, and my toothache is quite subsided; but I experience a loss of strength and a deficiency of spirit which would make me a sorry companion to you or anyone else. I would not be on a visit now for a large sum of money.

June, 1846.

I hope all the mournful contingencies of death are by this time removed from ——, and that some little sense of relief is beginning to be experienced by its wearied inmates. —— suffered greatly, I make no doubt; and I trust, and even believe, that his long sufferings on earth will be taken as sufficient expiation for his errors. One shudders for him, but it is his relations—his mother and sisters—whom I truly and permanently pity.

July 10th, 1846.

Dear Ellen,—Who gravely asked you whether Miss Brontë was not going to be married to ——? I scarcely need say that there never was rumour more unfounded. It puzzles me to think how it could possibly have originated.

A cold, far-away sort of civility, are the only terms on which I have ever been with Mr. ——. I could by no means think of mentioning such a rumour to him, even as a joke. It would make me the laughing-stock of himself and his fellow-curates, for half a year to come. They regard me as an old maid; and I regard them, one and all, as highly uninteresting, narrow, and unattractive specimens of the "coarser sex."

VII.

AUTHORSHIP AND BEREAVEMENT.

The reader has seen that it was not the degradation of Branwell Brontë which formed the turning-point in Charlotte's life. Mrs. Gaskell, anxious to support her own conception of what *should have been* Charlotte's feelings with regard to her brother's ruin, has scarcely done justice either to herself or to her heroine. Thus she makes use of a passage in one of the letters quoted in the foregoing chapter, but in doing so omits what are perhaps the most characteristic words in it. "He" (Branwell) "has written this morning expressing some sense of contrition; ... but as long as he remains at home I scarce dare hope for peace in the house." This is the form in which the passage appears in the "Biography," whereas Charlotte had written of her brother's having expressed "contrition for his frantic folly," and of his having "promised amendment on his return." Mrs. Gaskell could not bring herself to speak of such flagrant sins as those of which young Brontë had been guilty under the name of "folly," nor could she conceive that there was any possibility of amendment on the part of one who had fallen so low in vice. Moreover, one of her objects was to punish those who had shared the lad's misconduct, and to whom she openly attributed not only his ruin but the premature deaths of his sisters. Thus she felt compelled to take throughout her book a far deeper and more tragic view of this miserable episode in the Brontë story than Charlotte herself took. Having read all her letters written at this period of her life to her two most confidential friends, I am justified in saying that the impression produced on Charlotte by Branwell's degrading fall was not so deep as that which was produced on Mrs. Gaskell, who never saw young Brontë, by the mere recital of the story. Yet Charlotte, though too brave, healthy, and reasonable in all things to be utterly weighed down by the fact that her brother had fallen a victim to loathsome vice, was far from being insensible to the sadness and shamefulness of his condition. What she thought of it she has herself told the world in the story of "The Professor" (p. 198):

> Limited as had yet been my experience of life, I had once had the opportunity of contemplating near at hand an example of the results produced by a course of interesting and romantic domestic treachery. No golden halo of fiction was about this example; I saw it bare and real, and it was very loathsome. I saw a mind degraded by the practice of mean subterfuge, by the habit of perfidious deception, and a body depraved by the infectious influence of the vice-polluted soul. I had suffered much from the forced and prolonged view of this spectacle; those sufferings I did not now regret, for their simple recollection acted as a most wholesome antidote to temptation. They had inscribed on my reason the conviction that unlawful pleasure, trenching on another's rights, is delusive and envenomed pleasure—its hollowness disappoints at the time, its poison cruelly tortures afterwards, its effects deprave for ever.

Upon the gentle and sensitive mind of Anne Brontë the effect of Branwell's fall was such as Mrs. Gaskell depicts. She was literally broken down by the grief she suffered in seeing her brother's ruin; but Charlotte and Emily were of stronger fibre than their sister, and their predominant feeling, as expressed in their letters, is one of sheer disgust at their brother's weakness, and of indignation against all who had in any way assisted in his downfall. This may not be consistent with the popular conception of Charlotte's character, but it is strictly true.

We must then dismiss from our minds the notion that the brother's fate exercised that paramount influence over the sisters' lives which seems to be believed. Yet, as we have seen, there was a very strong though hidden influence working in Charlotte during those years in which their home was darkened by Branwell's presence. Her yearning for Brussels and the life that now seemed like a vanished dream, continued almost as strong as ever. At Haworth everything was dull, commonplace, monotonous. The school-keeping scheme had failed; poverty and obscurity seemed henceforth to be the appointed lot of all the sisters. Even the source of intercourse with friends was almost entirely cut off; for Charlotte could not bear the shame of exposing the prodigal of the family to the gaze of strangers. It was at this time, and in the mood described in the letters quoted in the preceding chapter, that she took up her pen, and sought to escape from the narrow and sordid cares which environed her by a flight into the region of poetry. She had been accustomed from childhood to write verses, few of which as yet had passed the limits of mediocrity. Now, with all that heart-history through which she had passed at Brussels weighing upon her, she began to write again, moved by a stronger impulse, stirred by deeper thoughts than any she had known before. In this secret exercise of her faculties she found relief and enjoyment; her letters to her friend showed that her mind was regaining its tone, and the dreary out-look from "the hills of Judæa" at Haworth began to brighten. It was a great day in the lives of all the sisters when Charlotte accidentally discovered that Emily also had dared to "commit her soul to paper." The younger sister was keenly troubled when Charlotte made the discovery, for her poems had been written in absolute secrecy. But mutual confessions hastened her reconcilement. Charlotte produced her own poems, and then Anne also, blushing as was her wont, poured some hidden treasures of the same kind into the eldest sister's lap. So it came to pass that in 1846, unknown to their nearest friends, they presented to the world—at their own cost and risk, poor souls!—that thin volume of poetry "by Currer, Ellis, and Acton Bell," now almost forgotten, the merits of which few readers have recognised and few critics proclaimed.

Strong, calm, sincere, most of these poems are; not the spasmodic or frothy outpourings of Byron-stricken girls; not even mere echoes, however skilful, of the grand music of the masters. When we dip into the pages of the book, we see that these women write because they feel. They write because they have something to say; they write not for the world, but for themselves, each sister wrapping her own secret within her own soul. Strangely enough, it is not Charlotte who carries off the palm in these poems. Verse seems to have been too narrow for the limits of her genius; she could not soar as she desired to do within the self-imposed restraints of rhythm, rhyme, and metre. Here and there, it is true, we come upon lines which flash upon us with the brilliant light of genius; but, upon the whole, we need not wonder that Currer Bell achieved no reputation as a poet. Nor is Anne to be counted among great singers. Sweet, indeed her verses are, radiant with the tenderness, resignation, and gentle humility which were the prominent features of her character. One or two of her little poems are now included in popular collections of hymns used in Yorkshire churches; but, as a rule, her compositions lack the vigorous life which belongs to those of her sisters. It is Emily who takes the first place in this volume. Some of her poems have a lyrical beauty which haunts the mind ever after it has become acquainted with them; others have a passionate emphasis, a depth of meaning, an intensity and gravity which are startling when we know who the singer is, and which furnish a key to many passages in "Wuthering Heights" which the world shudders at and hastily passes by. Such lines as these ought to make the name of Emily Brontë far more familiar than it is to the students of our modern English literature:

Death! that struck when I was most confiding
In my certain faith of joy to be—

Strike again, Time's withered branch dividing
From the fresh root of Eternity!

Leaves upon Time's branch were growing brightly,
Full of sap and full of silver dew;
Birds beneath its shelter gathered nightly;
Daily round its flowers the wild bees flew.

Sorrow passed, and plucked the golden blossom;
Guilt stripped off the foliage in its pride;
But within its parent's kindly bosom
Flowed for ever Life's restoring tide.

Little mourned I for the parted gladness,
For the vacant nest and silent song—
Hope was there, and laughed me out of sadness,
Whispering, "Winter will not linger long!"

And behold! with tenfold increase blessing,
Spring adorned the beauty-burdened spray;
Wind and rain and fervent heat, caressing,
Lavished glory on that second May!

High it rose—no winged grief could sweep it;
Sin was scared to distance by its shine;
Love, and its own life, had power to keep it
From all wrong—from every blight but thine,

Cruel Death! The young leaves droop and languish;
Evening's gentle air may still restore—
No! the morning sunshine mocks my anguish—
Time, for me, must never blossom more!

Strike it down, that other boughs may flourish
Where that perished sapling used to be;

Thus at least its mouldering corpse will nourish
That from which it sprung—Eternity.

The little book was a failure. This first flight ended only in discomfiture; and Currer, Ellis, and Acton Bell were once more left to face the realities of life in Haworth parsonage, uncheered by literary success. This was in the summer and autumn of 1846; about which time they were compelled to think of cares which came even nearer home than the failure of their volume of poems. Their father's eyesight was now almost gone, and all their thoughts were centred upon the operation which was to restore it. It was to Manchester that Mr. Brontë was taken by his daughters to undergo this operation. Many of the letters which were written by Charlotte at this period have already been published; but the two which I now quote are new, and they serve to show what were the narrow cares and anxieties which nipped the sisters at this eventful crisis in their lives:

September 22nd, 1846.

Dear Ellen,—I have nothing new to tell you, except that papa continues to do well, though the process of recovery appears to me very tedious. I daresay it will yet be many weeks before his sight is completely restored; yet every time Mr. Wilson comes, he expresses his satisfaction at the perfect success of the operation, and assures me papa will, ere long, be able both to read and write. He is still a prisoner in his darkened room, into which, however, a little more light is admitted than formerly. The nurse goes to-day—her departure will certainly be a relief, though she is, I daresay, not the worst of her class.

September 29th, 1846.

Dear Ellen,—When I wrote to you last, our return was uncertain indeed, but Mr. Wilson was called away to Scotland; his absence set us at liberty. I hastened our departure, and now we are at home. Papa is daily gaining strength. He cannot yet exercise his sight much, but it improves, and I have no doubt will continue to do so. I feel truly thankful for the good insured and the evil exempted during our absence. What you say about —— grieves me much, and surprises me too. I know well the malaria of ——, it is an abominable smell of gas. I was sick from it ten times a day while I stayed there. That they should hesitate to leave from scruples about furnishing new houses, provokes and amazes me. Is not the furniture they have very decent? The inconsistency of human beings passes belief. I wonder what their sister would say to them, if they told her that tale? She sits on a wooden stool without a back, in a log-house without a carpet, and neither is degraded nor thinks herself degraded by such poor accommodation.

HAWORTH PARSONAGE AND GRAVEYARD.

It was about the time when this journey to Manchester was first projected, and very shortly after they had become convinced that their poems were a failure, that the sisters embarked upon another and more important literary venture. The pen once taken up could not be laid down. By poetry they had only lost money; but the idea had occurred to them that by prose-writing money was to be made. At any rate, in telling the stories of imaginary people, in opening their hearts freely upon all those subjects on which they had thought deeply in their secluded lives, they would find relief from the solitude of Haworth. Each of the three accordingly began to write a novel. The stories were commenced simultaneously, after a long consultation, in which the outlines of the plots, and even the names of the different characters, were settled. How one must wish that some record of that strange literary council had been preserved! Charlotte, in after life, spoke always tenderly, lovingly, almost reverentially, of the days in which she and her well-beloved sisters were engaged in settling the plan and style of their respective romances. That time seemed sacred to her, and though she learnt to smile at the illusions under which the work was begun, and could see clearly enough the errors and crudities of thought and method which all three displayed, she never allowed any one in her presence to question the genius of Emily and Anne, or to ridicule the prosaic and business-like fashion in which the novel-writing was undertaken by the three sisters. Returning to the old customs of their childhood, they sat round the table of their sitting-room in the parsonage, each busy with her pen. No trace of their occupation at this time is to be found in their letters; and on the rare occasions on which the father or the brother came into their room, nothing was said as to the work that was going on. The novel-writing, like the writing and publishing of the poems, was still kept profoundly secret. "There is no gentleman of the name in this parish," said Mr. Brontë to the village postman, when the latter ventured to ask who the Mr. Currer Bell could be for whom letters came so frequently from London. But every night the three sisters, as they paced the barely-furnished room, or strained their eyes across the tombstones, to the spot where the weather-stained church-tower rose from a bank of nettles, told each other what the work of the day had been, and criticised each other's labours with the freedom of that perfect love which casts out all fear of misconception. And here I may interpolate two letters written whilst the novel-writing was in progress, which are in some respects not altogether insignificant:

> Dear Nell,—Your last letter both amused and edified me exceedingly. I could not but laugh at your account of the fall in B——, yet I should by no means have liked to have made a third party in that exhibition. I have endured one fall in your company, and undergone one of your ill-timed laughs, and don't wish to repeat my experience. Allow me to compliment you on the skill with which you can seem to give an explanation, without

enlightening one one whit on the question asked. I know no more about Miss R.'s superstition now, than I did before. What is the superstition?—about a dead body? And what is the inference drawn? Do you remember my telling you—or did I ever tell you—about that wretched and most criminal Mr. J. S.? After running an infamous career of vice, both in England and France, abandoning his wife to disease and total destitution in Manchester, with two children and without a farthing, in a strange lodging-house? Yesterday evening Martha came upstairs to say that a woman—"rather lady-like," as she said—wished to speak to me in the kitchen. I went down. There stood Mrs. S., pale and worn, but still interesting-looking, and cleanly and neatly dressed, as was her little girl who was with her. I kissed her heartily. I could almost have cried to see her, for I had pitied her with my whole soul when I heard of her undeserved sufferings, agonies, and physical degradation. She took tea with us, stayed about two hours, and frankly entered into the narrative of her appalling distresses. Her constitution has triumphed over her illness; and her excellent sense, her activity, and perseverance have enabled her to regain a decent position in society, and to procure a respectable maintenance for herself and her children. She keeps a lodging-house in a very eligible part of the suburbs of —— (which I know), and is doing very well. She does not know where Mr. S. is, and of course can never more endure to see him. She is now staying a few days at E——, with the ——s, who I believe have been all along very kind to her, and the circumstance is greatly to their credit.

I wish to know whether about Whitsuntide would suit you for coming to Haworth. We often have fine weather just then. At least I remember last year it was very beautiful at that season. Winter seems to have returned with severity on us at present, consequently we are all in the full enjoyment of a cold. Much blowing of noses is heard, and much making of gruel goes on in the house. How are you all?

May 12th, 1847.

Dear Ellen,—We shall all be glad to see you on the Thursday or Friday of next week, whichever day will suit you best. About what time will you be likely to get here, and how will you come—by coach to Keighley, or by a gig all the way to Haworth? There must be no impediments now. I could not do with them; I want very much to see you. I hope you will be decently comfortable while you stay. Branwell is quieter now, and for a good reason. He has got to the end of a considerable sum of money, of which he became possessed in the spring, and consequently is obliged to restrict himself in some degree. You must expect to find him weaker in mind, and the complete rake in appearance. I have no apprehension of his being at all uncivil to you, on the contrary he will be as smooth as oil.

I pray for fine weather, that we may be able to get out while you stay. Good-bye for the present. Prepare for much dulness and monotony. Give my love to all at B——.

Is it needful to tell how the three stories—"The Professor," "Wuthering Heights," and "Agnes Grey"—are sent forth at last from the little station at Keighley, to fare as best they may in that unknown London which is still an ideal city to the sisters, peopled not with ordinary human beings, but with creatures of some strangely-different order? Can any one be ignorant of the weary months which passed whilst "The Professor" was going from hand to hand, and the stories written by Emily and Anne were waiting in a publisher's desk until they could be given to the world on the publisher's own terms? Charlotte had failed, but the brave heart was not to be baffled. No sooner had the last page of "The Professor" been finished than the first page of "Jane Eyre" was begun. The whole of that wondrous story passed through the author's busy brain whilst the life around her was clad in these sombre hues, and disappointment, affliction, and gloomy forebodings were her daily companions. The decisive rejection of her first tale by Messrs. Smith, Elder, and Co. had been accompanied by some kindly words of advice; so it is to that firm that she now entrusts the completed manuscript of "Jane Eyre." The result has already been told. On August 24, 1847, the story is sent from Leeds to London; and before the year is out, all England is ringing with the praises of the novel and its author.

Need I defend the sisters from the charge sometimes brought against them that they were unfaithful to their friends in not taking them into their confidence? Surely not. They had pledged themselves to each other that the secret should be sternly guarded as something sacred, kept even from those of their own household. They were not working for fame; for again and again they give proof that personal fame is the last thing to which they aspire. But they had found their true vocation; the call to work was irresistible; they had obeyed it, and all that they sought now was to leave their work to speak for itself, dissevered absolutely from the humble personality of the authors.

In a letter from Anne Brontë, written in January, 1848, at which time the literary quidnuncs both of England and America were eagerly discussing contradictory theories as to the authorship of "Jane Eyre," and of the two other stories which had appeared from the pens of Ellis and Acton Bell, I find the following passage: "I have no news to tell you, for we have been nowhere, seen no one, and done nothing (to *speak* of) since you were here, and yet we contrive to be busy from morning till night." The gentle and scrupulously conscientious girl, whilst hiding the secret from her friend, cannot violate the truth even by a hairbreadth. The italics are her own. Nothing *that can be spoken of* has been done. The friend had her own suspicions. Staying in a southern house for the winter, the new novel about which everybody was talking was produced, fresh from town. One of the guests was deputed to read it aloud, and before she had proceeded far Charlotte Brontë's schoolfellow had pierced the secret of the authorship. Three months before, Charlotte had been spending a few days at Miss N――'s house, and had openly corrected the proof-sheets of the story in the presence of her hostess; but she had given the latter no encouragement to speak to her on the subject, and nothing had been said. Now, however, in the surprise of the moment, Miss N―― told the company that this must have been written by Miss Brontë; and astute friends at once advised her not to mention the fact that she knew the author of "Jane Eyre" to any one, as her acquaintance with such a person would be regarded as a reflection on her own character! When Charlotte was challenged by her friend, she uttered stormy denials in general terms, which carried a complete confirmation of the truth; and when, in the spring of 1848, Miss N―― visited Haworth, full confession was made, and the poems brought forth and shown to her, in addition to the stories.

Those who read Charlotte Brontë's letters will see that even before this avowal of her flight in authorship there is a distinct change in their tone. Not that she is less affectionate towards her early friend, or that she shows the smallest abatement of her interest in the fortunes of her old companions. On the contrary, it would almost seem as though the great event, which had altered the current of her life, had only served to bind her more closely than before to those whom she had known and loved in her obscurity. But there is a perceptible growth of power and independence in her mode of handling the topics, often trivial enough in themselves, which arise in any prolonged correspondence, which shows how much her mind had grown, how greatly her views had been enlarged, by the intellectual labours through which she had passed. The following was the last letter written by her to her schoolfellow whilst the authorship of "Jane Eyre" was still a secret, and it will, I think, bear out what I have said:

April 25th, 1848.

I was not at all surprised at the contents of your note. Indeed, what part of it was new to us? V—— has his good and bad side, like most others. There is his own original nature, and there are the alterations the world has made in him. Meantime, why do B—— and G—— trouble themselves with matching him? Let him, in God's name, court half the country-side and marry the other half, if such procedure seem good in his eyes, and let him do it all in quietness. He has his own botherations, no doubt; it does not seem to be such very easy work getting married, even for a man, since it is necessary to make up to so many ladies. More tranquil are those who have settled their bargain with celibacy. I like Q——'s letters more and more. Her goodness is indeed better than mere talent. I fancy she will never be married, but the amiability of her character will give her comfort. To be sure, one has only her letters to judge from, and letters often deceive; but hers seem so artless and unaffected. Still, were I in your place I should feel uneasy in the midst of this correspondence. Does a doubt of mutual satisfaction in case you should one day meet never torment you?... Anne says it pleases her to think that you have kept her little drawing. She would rather have done it for you than for a stranger.

Very quietly and sedately did "Currer Bell" take her sudden change of fortune. She corresponded freely with her publishers, and with the critics who had written to her concerning her book; she told her father the secret of her authorship, and exhibited to him the draft which was the substantial recompense of her labours; but in her letters to her friend no difference of tone is to be detected. Success was very sweet to her, as we know; but she bore her honours meekly, betraying nothing of the gratified ambition which must have filled her soul. She had not even revealed her identity to the publisher till, by an accident, she became aware of the rumour that the writer had satirised Mr. Thackeray under the character of Rochester, and had even obtruded on the sorrows of his private life. Shocked at this supposition, she went to London by the night train, accompanied by Anne, and having breakfasted at the station, walked to the establishment in Cornhill, where she had much difficulty in penetrating to the head of the house, having stated that he would not know her by her name. At last he came into the shop, saying, with some annoyance: "Young woman, what can you want with me?" "Sir, we have come up from Yorkshire. I wish to speak to you privately. I wrote 'Jane Eyre.'" "*You* wrote 'Jane Eyre!'" cried the delighted publisher; and taking them into his office, insisted on their coming to the house of his mother, who would take every care of them. Charlotte related afterwards the strange contrast between the desolate waiting at the station in the early morning, and their loneliness in the crowd of the great city, and finding themselves in the evening seated among the brilliant company at the Opera House, listening to the performance of Jenny Lind.

But her thoughts were soon turned from her literary triumphs. Branwell, who had been so long the dark shadow in their "humble home," was taken from them without any lengthened preliminary warning. Sharing to the full the eccentricity of the family, he resolved to die as nobody else had ever died before; and when the last agony came on he rose to his feet, as though proudly defying death itself to do its worst, and expired standing. In the following letter, hitherto unpublished, to one of her friends—not to her old schoolfellow—Charlotte thus speaks of the last act in the tragedy of her brother's life:

Haworth, October 14th, 1848.

The event to which you allude came upon us indeed with startling suddenness, and was a severe shock to us all. My poor brother has long had a shaken constitution, and during the summer his appetite had been diminished and he had seemed weaker; but neither we, nor himself, nor any medical man who was consulted on his case, thought it one of immediate danger: he was out of doors two days before his death, and was only confined to bed one single day. I thank you for your kind sympathy. Many, under the circumstances, would think our loss rather a relief than otherwise; in truth, we must acknowledge, in all humility and gratitude, that God has greatly tempered judgment with mercy; but yet, as you doubtless know from experience, the last earthly separation cannot take place between near relations without the keenest pangs on the part of the survivors. Every wrong and sin is forgotten then; pity and grief share the heart and the memory between them. Yet we are not without comfort in our affliction. A most propitious change marked the few last days of poor Branwell's life; his demeanour, his language, his sentiments, were all singularly altered and softened, and this change could not be owing to the fear of death, for within half an hour of his decease he seemed unconscious of danger. In God's hands we leave him! He sees not as man sees. Papa, I am thankful to say, has borne the event pretty well. His distress was great at first. To lose an only son is no ordinary trial. But his physical strength has not hitherto failed him, and he has now in a great measure recovered his mental composure; my dear sisters are pretty well also. Unfortunately illness attacked me at the crisis, when strength was most needed; I bore up for a day or two, hoping to be better, but got worse; fever, sickness, total loss of appetite and internal pain were the symptoms. The doctor pronounced it to be bilious fever—but I think it must have been in a mitigated form; it yielded to medicine and care in a few days; I was only confined to my bed a week, and am, I trust, nearly well now. I felt it a grievous thing to be incapacitated from action and effort at a time when action and effort were most called for. The past month seems an overclouded period in my life.

Alas! the brave woman who felt it to be "a grievous thing" that she could not bear her full share of the family burden, little knew how terribly that burden was to be increased, how much heavier and blacker were the clouds which awaited her than any through which she had yet passed. The storm which even then was gathering upon her path was one which no sunshine of fame or prosperity could dissipate. The one to whom Charlotte's heart had always clung most fondly, the sister who had been nearest to her in age and nearest to her in affection, Emily, the brilliant but ill-fated child of genius, began to fade. "She had never," says Charlotte, speaking in the solitude of her fame, "lingered over any task in her life, and she did not linger now." Yet the quick decline of Emily Brontë is one of the saddest of all the sad features of the story. I have spoken of her reserve. So intense was it that when dying she refused to admit even to her own sisters that she was ill. They saw her fading before their eyes; they knew that the grave was yawning at her feet; and yet they dared not offer her any attention such as an invalid needed, and such as they were longing to bestow upon her. It was the cruellest torture of Charlotte's life. During the brief period of Emily's illness, her sister writes as follows to her friend:

> I mentioned your coming to Emily as a mere suggestion, with the faint hope that the prospect might cheer her, as she really esteems you perhaps more than any other person out of this house. I found, however, it would not do; any,

the slightest excitement or putting out of the way, is not to be thought of, and indeed I do not think the journey in this unsettled weather, with the walk from Keighley and back, at all advisable for yourself. Yet I should have liked to see you, and so would Anne. Emily continues much the same: yesterday I thought her a little better, but to-day she is not so well. I hope still, for I *must* hope; she is as dear to me as life. If I let the faintness of despair reach my heart I shall become worthless. The attack was, I believe, in the first place, inflammation of the lungs; it ought to have been met promptly in time; but she would take no care, use no means, she is too intractable. I *do* wish I knew her state and feelings more clearly. The fever is not so high as it was, but the pain in the side, the cough, the emaciation are there still.

The days went by in the parsonage, slowly, solemnly, each bringing some fresh burden of sorrow to the broken hearts of Charlotte and Anne. Emily's resolute spirit was unbending to the last. Day after day she refused to own that she was ill, refused to take rest or medicine or stimulants; compelled her trembling hands to labour as of old. And so came the bitter morning in December, the story of which has been told by Mrs. Gaskell with simple pathos, when she "arose and dressed herself as usual, making many a pause, but doing everything for herself," even going on with her sewing as at any time during the years past; until suddenly she laid the unfinished work aside, whispered faintly to her sister: "If you send for a doctor I will see him now," and in two hours passed quietly away.

The broken father, supported on either side by his surviving daughters, followed Emily to her grave in the old church. There was one other mourner—the fierce old dog whom she had loved better almost than any human being.

Yes—says Charlotte, writing to her friend—there is no

Emily in time or on earth now. Yesterday we put her poor wasted mortal frame quietly under the church pavement. We are very calm at present. Why should we be otherwise? The anguish of seeing her suffer is over. We feel she is at peace. No need now to tremble for the hard frost and the keen wind. Emily does not feel them. She died in a time of promise. We saw her taken from life in its prime. But it is God's will, and the place where she is gone is better than that she has left.

It was in the very month of December, 1848, when Charlotte passed through this fierce ordeal, and wrote these tender words of love and resignation, that the *Quarterly Review* denounced her as an improper woman, who "for some sufficient reason" had forfeited the society of her sex!

Terrible was the storm of death which in three short months swept off two of the little household at Haworth; but it had not even yet exhausted all its fury. Scarcely had Emily been laid in the grave than Anne, the youngest and gentlest of the three sisters, began to fade. Very slowly did she droop. The winter passed away, and the spring came with a glimmer of hope; but the following unpublished letter, written on the 16th of May, shows with what fears Charlotte set forth on that visit to Scarborough which her sister insisted upon undertaking as a last resource:

Next Wednesday is the day fixed for our departure; Ellen accompanies us at her own kind and friendly wish. I would not refuse her society, but dared not urge her to go, for I have little hope that the excursion will be one of pleasure or benefit to those engaged in it. Anne is extremely weak. She herself has a fixed impression that the sea-air will give her a chance of regaining strength. That chance therefore she must have. Having resolved to try the experiment, misgivings are useless, and yet when I look at her misgivings will rise. She is more emaciated than Emily was at the very last, her breath scarcely serves her to mount the stairs, however slowly. She sleeps very little at night, and often passes most of the forenoon in a semi-lethargic state. Still she is up all day, and even goes out a little when it is fine. Fresh air usually acts as a temporary stimulus, but its reviving power diminishes.

I am indebted to the faithful friend and companion to whom allusion is made above, for the following account of the sad journey to Scarborough, and of its tragic end:

> On our way to Scarborough we stopped at York, and after a rest at the George Hotel, and partaking of dinner, which she enjoyed, Anne went out in a bath-chair, and made purchases, along with Charlotte, of bonnets and dresses, besides visiting the minister. The morning after her arrival at Scarborough, she insisted on going to the baths, and would be left there with only the attendant in charge. She walked back alone to her lodgings, but fell exhausted as she reached the garden-gate. She never named this, but it was discovered afterwards. The same day she had a drive in a donkey carriage, and talked with the boy-driver on kindness to animals. On Sunday she wanted again to be left alone, and for us to go to church. Finding we would not leave her, she begged that she might go out, and we walked down towards the saloon, she resting half way, and sending us on with the excuse that she wanted us to see the place, this being *our* first visit, though not hers. In the evening, after again asking us to go to church, she sat by the sitting-room window, enjoying a very glorious sunset. Next morning (the day she died) she rose by seven o'clock and dressed herself, refusing all assistance. She was the first of the little party to be ready to go downstairs; but when she reached the head of the stairs, she felt fearful of descending. Charlotte

went to her and discovered this. I fancying there was some difficulty, left my room to see what it was, when Anne smilingly told me she felt afraid of the steps downward. I immediately said: "Let me try to carry you;" she looked pleased, but feared for me. Charlotte was angry at the idea, and greatly distressed, I could see, at this new evidence of Anne's weakness. Charlotte was at last persuaded to go to her room and leave us. I then went a step or two below Anne, and begged her to put her arms round my neck, and I said: "I will carry you like a baby." She still feared, but on my promising to put her down if I could not do it, she consented to trust herself to me. Strength seemed to be given for the effort, but on reaching the foot of the stairs, poor Anne's head fell like a leaden weight upon the top of mine. The shock was terrible, for I felt it could only be death that was coming. I just managed to bear her to the front of her easy-chair and drop her into it, falling myself on my knees before her, very miserable at the fact, and letting her fall at last, though it was into her chair. She was shaken, but she put out her arms to comfort me, and said: "You know it could not be helped, you did your best." After this she sat at the breakfast-table and partook of a basin of boiled milk prepared for her. As 11 a.m. approached, she wondered if she could be conveyed home in time to die there. At 2 p.m. death had come, and left only her beautiful form in the sweetest peace.

She rendered up her soul with that sweetness and resignation of spirit which had adorned her throughout her brief life, even in the last hour crying: "Take courage, Charlotte, take courage!" as she bade farewell to the sister who was left.

Before me lie the few letters which remain of Emily and Anne. There is little in them worth preserving. Both make reference to the fact that Charlotte is the great correspondent of the family, and that their brief and uninteresting epistles can have no charm for one who is constantly receiving letters from her. Yet that modest reserve which distinguished the greatest of the three is plainly visible in what little remains of the correspondence of the others. They had discovered before their death the real power that lay within them; they had just experienced the joy which comes from the exercise of this power; they had looked forward to a future which should be sunny and prosperous, as no other part of their lives of toil and patient endurance had been. Suddenly death had confronted them, and they recognised the fact that they must leave their work undone. Each faced the dread enemy in her own way, but neither shrank even from that blow. Emily's proud spirit refused to be conquered, and, as we have seen, up to the last agony she carried herself as one sternly indifferent to the weaknesses of the flesh, including that final weakness which must conquer all of us in the end. Anne found consolation, pure and deep, in her religious faith, and she died cheerfully in the firm belief that she was but entering upon that fuller life which lay beyond the grave. The one was defiant, the other resigned; but courage and fortitude were shown by each in accordance with her own special idiosyncrasy.

VIII.

"SHIRLEY."

Charlotte went back from Scarborough to Haworth alone. Her father met her with unwonted demonstrations of affection, and she "tried to be glad" that she was once more under the familiar roof. "But this time joy was not to be the sensation." Yet the courage which had held her sisters to the end supported her amid the pangs of loneliness and bereavement. Even now there was no bitterness, no morbid gloom in the heart which had suffered so keenly. Quietly but resolutely setting aside her own sorrow, refusing all the invitations of her friend to seek temporary relief in change of scene, she sat down to complete the story which was intended to tell the world what the lost Emily had seemed to be in the eyes of her fond sister. By herself, in the room in which a short year ago three happy sisters had worked together, within the walls which could never again echo with the old voices, or walking on the moors, which would never more be trodden by the firm, elastic step of Emily, she composed the brilliant story of "Shirley"—the brightest and healthiest of her works. As she writes she sometimes sends forth messages to those who love her, which tell us of the spirit of the hero or the martyr burning within the frail frame of the solitary woman. "Submission, courage, exertion when practicable—these seem to be the weapons with which we must fight life's long battle;" and that these are no mere words she proves with all her accustomed honesty and sincerity, by acting up to them to the very letter. But at times the burden presses upon her till it is almost past endurance. Strangely enough, it is a comparative trifle, as the world counts it, the illness of a servant, that occasions her fiercest outburst of open grief:

> You have to fight your way through labour and difficulty at home, it appears, but I am truly glad now you did not come to Haworth. As matters have turned out you would have found only discomfort and gloom. Both Tabby and Martha are at this moment ill in bed. Martha's illness has been most serious. She was seized with internal inflammation ten days ago; Tabby's lame leg has broken out, she cannot stand or walk. I have one of Martha's sisters to help me, and her mother comes up sometimes. There was one day last week when I fairly broke down for ten minutes, and sat down and cried like a fool. Martha's illness was at its height; a cry from Tabby had called me into the kitchen, and I had found her laid on the floor, her head under the kitchen-grate. She had fallen from her chair in attempting to rise. Papa had just been declaring that Martha was in imminent danger; I was myself depressed with headache and sickness that day; I hardly knew what to do or where to turn. Thank God, Martha is now convalescent; Tabby, I trust, will be better soon. Papa is pretty well. I have the satisfaction of knowing that my publishers are delighted with what I sent them—this supports me, but life is a battle. May we *all* be enabled to fight it well.

This letter is dated September 24, 1849, at which time "Shirley" is written, and in the hands of her publishers. She has painted the character of Emily in that of Shirley herself; and her friend Ellen is shadowed forth to the world in the person of Caroline Helston. When the book, with its vivid pictures of Yorkshire life at the beginning of the century, and its masterly sketches of characters as real as those which Shakespeare brings upon the stage, is published, there is but one outcry of praise, even from the critics who were so eager to condemn "Jane Eyre." Up to this point she had preserved her anonymity, but now she is discovered, and her admirers in London persuade her at last to visit them, and make acquaintance with her peers in the Republic of Letters, the men and women whose names were household words in Haworth Parsonage long before "Currer Bell" had made her first modest appeal to the world.

THE "FIELD HEAD" OF SHIRLEY.

A passage from one of the following letters, written during this first sojourn in London, has already been published; but it will well bear reprinting:

December, 1849.

I have just remembered that as you do not know my address you cannot write to me till you get it. I came to this big Babylon last Thursday, and have been in what seems to me a sort of whirl ever since; for changes, scenes, and stimulus, which would be a trifle to others, are much to me. I found when I mentioned to Mr. —— my plan of going to Dr. ——'s it would not do at all. He would have been seriously hurt: he made his mother write to me, and thus I was persuaded to make my principal stay at his house. So far I have found no reason to regret this decision. Mrs. —— received me at first like one who has had the strictest orders to be scrupulously attentive. I had fire in my bedroom evening and morning, two wax candles, &c., and Mrs. —— and her daughters seemed to look on me with a mixture of respect and alarm. But all this is changed; that is to say, the attention and politeness continue as great as ever, but the alarm and estrangement are quite gone; she treats me as if she liked me, and I begin to like her much. Kindness is a potent heart-winner. I had not judged too favourably of —— on a first impression—he pleases me much: I like him better as a son and brother than as a man of business. Mr. W—— too is really most gentlemanly and well-informed; his weak points he certainly has, but these are not seen in society. Mr. X—— (the little man) has again shown his parts. Of him I have not yet come to a clear decision. Abilities he has, for he rules his firm and keeps forty young men under strict control by his iron will. His young superior likes him, which, to speak the truth, is more than I do at present. In fact, I suspect that he is of the Helston order of men—rigid, despotic, and self-willed. He tries to be very kind, and even to express sympathy sometimes, and he does not manage it. He has a determined, dreadful nose in the middle of his face, which, when poked into my countenance, cuts into my soul like iron. Still he is horribly intelligent, quick, searching, sagacious, and with a memory of relentless tenacity: to turn to—after him is to turn from granite to easy down or warm fur. I have seen Thackeray.

As to being happy, I am under scenes and circumstances

of excitement, but I suffer acute pain sometimes—mental pain, I mean. At the moment Mr. Thackeray presented himself I was thoroughly faint from inanition, having eaten nothing since a very slight breakfast, and it was then seven o'clock in the evening. Excitement and exhaustion together made savage work of me that evening. What he thought of me I cannot tell. This evening I am going to meet Miss Martineau; she has written to me most kindly; she knows me only as Currer Bell; I am going alone; how I shall get on I do not know. If Mrs. —— were not kind, I should sometimes be miserable; but she treats me almost affectionately, her attentions never flag. I have seen many things; I hope some day to tell you what. Yesterday I went over the new Houses of Parliament with Mr. ——. An attack of rheumatic fever has kept poor Mr. X—— out of the way since I wrote last. I am sorry for *his* sake. It grows quite dark. I must stop. I shall not stay in London a day longer than I first intended. On those points I form my resolutions, and will not be shaken. The thundering *Times* has attacked me savagely.

The following letters (with one exception not previously published) belong to the spring of 1850, when Charlotte was at home again, engaged in attending to her father and to the household cares which shared her attention with literary work and anxieties. The first, which refers exclusively to her visit to London, was addressed to one of her old friends in Yorkshire:

Ellen it seems told you that I spent a fortnight in London last December. They wished me very much to stay a month, alleging that I should in that time be able to secure a complete circle of acquaintance, but I found a fortnight of such excitement quite enough. The whole day was usually devoted to sight-seeing, and often the evening was spent in society; it was more than I could bear for any length of time. On one occasion I met a party of my critics—seven of them. Some of them had been my bitter foes in print, but they were prodigiously civil face to face. These gentlemen seemed infinitely grander, more pompous, dashing, showy, than the few authors I saw. Mr. Thackeray, for example, is a man of very quiet, simple demeanour; he is, however, looked upon with some awe and even distrust. His conversation is very peculiar, too perverse to be pleasant. It was proposed to me to see Charles Dickens, Lady Morgan, Mesdames Trollope, Gore, and some others; but I was aware these introductions would bring a degree of notoriety I was not disposed to encounter; I declined therefore with thanks. Nothing charmed me more during my stay in town than the pictures I saw; one or two private collections of Turner's best water-colours were indeed a treat. His later oil paintings are strange things—things that baffle description. I have twice seen Macready act; once in "Macbeth," and once in "Othello." I astounded a dinner-party by honestly saying I did not like him. It is the fashion to rave about his splendid acting; anything more false and artificial, less genuinely impressive than his whole style, I could scarcely have imagined. The fact is, the stage system altogether is hollow nonsense. They act farces well enough; the actors comprehend their parts and do them justice. They comprehend nothing about tragedy or Shakespeare, and it is a failure. I said so, and by so saying produced a blank silence, a mute consternation. I was indeed obliged to dissent on many occasions, and to offend by dissenting. It seems now very much the custom to admire a certain wordy, intricate, obscure style of poetry, such as Elizabeth Barrett Browning writes. Some pieces were referred to, about which Currer Bell was expected to be very rapturous, and failing in this he disappointed. London people strike a provincial as being very much taken up with little matters, about which no one out of particular town circles cares much. They talk too of persons, literary men and women, whose names are scarcely heard in the country, and in whom you cannot get up an interest. I think I should scarcely like to live in London, and were I obliged to live there I should certainly go little into company—especially I should eschew the literary critics.

I have, since you went, had a remarkable epistle from Thackeray, long, interesting, characteristic; but it unfortunately concludes with the strict injunction, *Show this letter to no one*; adding that if he thought his letters were seen by others, he would either cease to write, or write only what was conventional. But for this circumstance I should have sent it with the others. I answered it at length. Whether my reply will give satisfaction or displeasure remains yet to be ascertained. Thackeray's feelings are not such as can be gauged by ordinary calculation: variable weather is what I should ever expect from that quarter. Yet in correspondence, as in verbal intercourse, this would torment me.

THE "BRIARFIELD" CHURCH OF SHIRLEY.

I believe I should have written to you before, but I don't know what heaviness of spirit has beset me of late, made my faculties dull, made rest weariness, and occupation burdensome. Now and then the silence of the house, the solitude of the room has pressed on me with a weight I found it difficult to bear, and recollection has not failed to be as alert, poignant, obtrusive, as other feelings were languid. I attribute this state of things partly to the weather. Quicksilver invariably falls low in storms and high winds, and I have ere this been warned of approaching disturbance in the atmosphere by a sense of bodily weakness, and deep, heavy mental sadness, which some would call *presentiment*. Presentiment indeed it is, but not at all supernatural. The Haworth people have been making great fools of themselves about "Shirley;" they take it in the enthusiastic light. When they got the volumes at the Mechanics' Institution, all the members wanted them; they cast lots for the whole three, and whoever got a volume was only allowed to keep it two days, and to be fined a shilling *per diem* for longer detention. It would be mere nonsense and vanity to tell you what they say. I have had no letters from London for a long time, and am very much ashamed of myself to find, now that that stimulus is withdrawn, how dependent upon it I had become. I cannot help feeling something of the excitement of expectation till post-hour comes, and when day after day it brings nothing I get low. This is a stupid, disgraceful, unmeaning state of things. I feel bitterly enraged at my own dependence and folly. It is so bad for the mind to be quite alone, to have none with whom to talk over little crosses and disappointments, and laugh them away. If I could write I daresay I should be better, but I cannot write a line. However (D. V.), I shall contend against the idiocy. I had rather a foolish letter from Miss —— the other day. Some things in it nettled me, especially an unnecessarily earnest assurance that in spite of all I had gone and done in the writing line I still retained a place in her esteem. My answer took strong and high ground at once. I said I had been troubled by no doubts on the subject, that I neither did myself nor her the injustice to suppose there was anything in what I had written to incur the just forfeiture of esteem. I was aware, I intimated, that some persons thought proper to take exceptions at "Jane Eyre," and that for their own sakes I was sorry, as I invariably found them individuals in whom the animal largely predominated over the intellectual, persons by nature coarse, by inclination sensual, whatever they might be by education and principle.

I enclose a slip of newspaper for your amusement. Me it both amused and touched, for it alludes to some who are in this world no longer. It is an extract from an American paper, and is written by an emigrant from Haworth. You will find it a curious mixture of truth and inaccuracy. Return it when you write again. I also send you for perusal an opinion of "Jane Eyre," written by a *working man* in this village; rather, I should say, a record of the feelings the book excited in the poor fellow's mind; it was not written for my inspection, nor does the writer now know that his little document has by intricate ways come into my possession, and I have forced those who gave it to promise that they will never inform him of this circumstance. He is a modest, thoughtful, feeling, reading being, to whom I have spoken perhaps about three times in the course of my life; his delicate health renders him incapable of hard or close labour; he and his family are often under the pressure of want. He feared that if Miss Brontë saw what he had written she would laugh it to scorn. But Miss Brontë considers it one of the highest, because one of the most truthful and artless tributes her work has yet received. You must return this likewise. I do you great honour in showing it to you.

Once more we can see that the healthy, happy interest she takes in the welfare of others is beginning to assert itself. For a time, under the keen smart of the wounds death had inflicted on her, she had found little heart to discuss the affairs of her circle of friends in her correspondence; but now the outer world vindicates its claim to her renewed attention, and she again begins to discuss and analyse the characters of her acquaintances with a skill and minuteness which make them as interesting even to strangers as any of the most closely-studied characters of fiction can be.

I return Q——'s letter. The business is a most unpleasant one to be concerned in. It seems to me *now* altogether unworthy in its beginning, progress, and ending. Q—— is the only pure thing about it; she stands between her coarse father and cold, unloving suitor, like innocence between a pair of world-hardened knaves. The comparison seems rather hard to be applied to V——, but as I see him now he merits it. If V—— has no means of keeping a wife, if he does not possess a sixpence he is sure of, how can he think of marrying a woman from whom he cannot expect she should work to keep herself? V——'s want of candour, the twice-falsified account he gave of the matter, tells painfully and deeply against him. It shows a glimpse of his hidden motives such as I refrain from describing in words. After all he is perhaps only like the majority of men. Certainly those men who lead a gay life in their youth, and arrive at middle life with feelings blunted and passions exhausted, can have but one aim in marriage—the selfish advancement of their interest. And to think that such men take as wives—as second selves—women young, modest, sincere, pure in heart and life, with feelings all fresh and emotions all unworn, and bind such virtue and vitality to their own withered existence, such sincerity to their own hollowness, such disinterestedness to their own haggard avarice! to think this, troubles the soul to its inmost depths. Nature and justice forbid the banns of such wedlock. This note is written under excitement. Q——'s letter seems to have lifted so fraudulent a veil, and to show both father and suitor lurking behind in shadow so dark, acting from motives so poor and low, so conscious of each other's littleness, and consequently so destitute of mutual respect! These things incense me, but I shall cool down.

I cannot find your last letter to refer to, and therefore this will be no answer to it. You must write again by return of post if possible, and let me know how you are progressing. What you said in your last confirmed my opinion that your late attack had been coming on for a long time. Your wish for a cold-water bath, &c, is, I should think, the result of fever. Almost everyone has complained lately of some tendency to slow fever. I have felt it in frequent thirst and in frequent appetite. Papa too, and even Martha, have complained. I fear this damp weather will scarcely suit you; but write and say all. Of late I have had many letters to answer; and some very bothering ones from people who want opinions about their books, who seek acquaintance, and who flatter to get it; people who utterly mistake all about me. They are most difficult to answer, put off, and appease, without offending; for such characters are excessively touchy, and when affronted turn malignant. Their books are too often deplorable.

In June, 1850, she is induced to pay another visit to London, going upon this occasion whilst the season is at its height, though she has stipulated before going that she is "not to be lionised."

I came to London last Thursday. I am staying at ——. Here I feel very comfortable. Mrs. —— treats me with a serene, equable kindness which just suits me. Her son is as before—genial and friendly. I have seen very few persons, and am not likely to see many, as the agreement was that I was to be very quiet. We have been to the exhibition of the Royal Academy, to the opera, and the Zoological Gardens. The weather is splendid. I shall not stay longer than a fortnight in London; the feverishness and exhaustion beset me somewhat, but I think not quite so badly as before—as indeed I have not yet been so much tired.

I am leaving London if all be well on Tuesday, and shall be very glad to come to you for a few days if that arrangement still remains convenient to you. My London visit has much surpassed my expectations this time. I have suffered less, and enjoyed more than before; rather a trying termination yet remains to me. Mrs. ——'s youngest son is at school in Scotland, and her eldest is going to fetch him home for the vacation. The other evening he announced his intention of taking one of his sisters with him, and the evening after he further proposed that Miss Brontë should go down to Edinburgh and join them there, and see that city and its suburbs. I concluded he was joking, laughed and declined. However, it seems he was in earnest, and being always accustomed to have his will, he brooks opposition ill. The thing appearing to me perfectly out of the question, I still refused. Mrs. —— did not at all favour it, but her worthy son only waxed more determined. This morning she came and entreated me to go; G—— wished it so much, he had begged her to use her influence, &c. &c. Now, I believe that he and I understand each other very well, and respect each other very sincerely. We both know the wide breach time has made between us. We do not embarrass each other, or very rarely. My six or eight years of seniority, to say nothing of lack of all pretensions to beauty, &c, are a perfect safeguard. I should not in the least fear to go with him to China. I like to see him pleased. I greatly *dis*like to ruffle and disappoint him; so he shall have his mind, and if all be well I mean to join him in Edinburgh, after I have spent a few days with you. With his buoyant animal spirits and youthful vigour he will make severe demands on my muscles and nerves; but I daresay I shall get through somehow.

IX.

LONELINESS AND FAME.

Charlotte Brontë's letters during 1850 and 1851 are among the most valuable illustrations of the true character of the woman which we possess. Stricken as she had been by successive bereavements, which had robbed her of her dearest friends and companions, and left her the sole prop of the dull house on the moors and of its aged head, she had yet recovered much of her peace of mind and even of her vitality and cheerfulness. She had now, also, begun to see something of life as it is presented, not to despised governesses, but to successful authoresses. Her visits to London had brought her into contact with some of the leaders of the literary world. Who can have forgotten her interview with Thackeray, when she was "moved to speak to the giant of some of his shortcomings?" Haworth itself had become a point of attraction to curious persons, and not a few visitors found their way under one pretence or another to the old parsonage, to be received with effusive courtesy by Mr. Brontë, and with shy indifference by his daughter. Her correspondence, too, became widely-spread among men and women of distinction in the world and in Society. Altogether it was a different life upon which she now looked out from her remote eyrie among the hills—a life with many new interests in it, with much that was calculated to awaken chords in her heart hitherto untouched, and to bring to light new characteristics of her temper and genius. One would fain speculate upon what might have been, but for the desolation wrought in her home and heart by that tempest of death which raged during the autumn of 1848 and the spring of 1849. As it was, no novelty could make her forget what had been; no new faces, however welcome, could dim the tender visions of the faces that were seen no more, or could weaken in any degree the affection with which she still clung to the friend of her school-days. Simplicity and sincerity are the prevailing features of her letters, during this critical time in her life, as during all the years which had preceded it. They reflect her mind in many moods; they show her in many different situations; but they never fail to give the impression of one whose allegiance to her own conscience and whose reverence for truth and purity remain now what they had been in her days of happy and unworldly obscurity. The letters I now quote are quite new to the public.

July 18th, 1850.

You must cheer up, for your letter proves to me that you are low-spirited. As for me, what I said is to be taken in this sense: that, under the circumstances, it would be presumptuous in me to calculate on a long life—a truth obvious enough. For the rest, we are all in the hands of Him who apportions His gifts, health or sickness, length or brevity of days, as is best for the receiver: to him who has work to do time will be given in which to do it; for him to whom no task is assigned the season of rest will come earlier. As to the suffering preceding our last sleep, the sickness, decay, the struggle of flesh and spirit, it *must* come sooner or later to all. If, in one point of view, it is sad to have few ties in the world, in another point of view it is soothing; women who have husbands and children must look forward to death with more pain, more fear, than those who have none. To dismiss the subject, I wish (without cant, and not in any hackneyed sense) that both you and I could always say in this matter, the will of God be done. I am beginning to get settled at home, but the solitude seems heavy as yet. It is a great change, but in looking forward I try to hope for the best. So little faith have I in the power of any temporary excitement to do real good that I put off day by day writing to London to tell them I have come home; and till then it was agreed I should not hear from them. It is painful to be dependent on the small stimulus letters give. I sometimes think I will renounce it altogether, close all correspondence on some quiet pretext, and cease to look forward at post-time for any letters but yours.

August 1st, 1850.

My dear E.,—I have certainly felt the late wet weather a good deal, and been somewhat bothered with frequently-returning colds, and so has Papa. About him I have been far from happy: every cold seems to make and leave him so weak. It is easy to say this world is only a scene of probation, but it is a hard thing to feel. Your friends the ——s seem to be happy just now, and long may they continue to be so! Give C. Brontë's sincere love to R—— and tell her she hopes Mr. —— will make her a good husband. If he does not, woe be to him! I wish a similar wish for Q——; and then I do really think there will be a kind of happiness. That proposition about remaining at H—— sounds like beginning life sensibly, with no showy dash—I like it. Are you comfortable amongst all these turtle-doves? I could not maintain your present position for a day; I should feel *de trop*, as the French say; that is in the way. But you are different to me. My portrait is come from London, and the Duke of Wellington's, and kind letters enough. Papa thinks the portrait looks older than I do. He says the features are far from flattered, but acknowledges that the expression is wonderfully good and life-like. I left the book called "Social Aspects" at B——; accept it from me. I may well give it you, for the author has kindly sent me another copy.... You ask for some promise: who that does not know the future can make promises? Not I.

September 2nd, 1850.

Poor Mrs. A—— it seems is gone; I saw her death in the papers. It is another lesson on the nature of life, on its strange brevity, and in many instances apparent futility.... V—— came here on Saturday last; T——, who was to have accompanied him, was prevented from executing his intention. I regretted his absence, for I by no means coveted the long *tête-à-tête* with V——. However, it passed off pretty well. He is satisfied now with his own prospects, and this makes him—on the surface—satisfied with other things. He spoke of Q—— with content and approbation. He looks forward to marriage as a sort of harbour where he is to lay up his now somewhat battered vessel in quiet moorings. He has seen all he wants to see of life; now he is prepared to settle. I listened to all with equanimity and cheerfulness—not assumed but real—for Papa is now somewhat better; his appetite and spirits are improved, and that eases my mind of cankering anxiety. My own health, too, is, I think, really benefited by the late changes of air and scene; I fancy, at any rate, that I feel stronger. Still I mused in my own way on V——'s character—its depth and scope, I believe, are ascertained.

I saw the governess at ——; she looked a little better and more cheerful. She was almost as pleased to see me as if we had been related; and when I bid her good-bye expressed an earnest hope that I would soon come again. The children seem fond of her, and on the whole obedient—two great alleviations of the inevitable evils of her position.

Cheer up, dear Nell, and try not to stagnate; or, when you cannot help it, and when your heart is constricted and oppressed, remember what life is and must be to all: some moments of sunshine alternating with many of overclouded and often tempestuous darkness. Humanity cannot escape its fate, which is to drink a mixed cup. Let us believe that the gall and the vinegar are salutary.

Sept. 14th, 1850.

I wish, dear Ellen, you would tell me what is the "twaddle" about my marrying, which you hear. If I knew the details I should have a better chance of guessing the quarter from which such gossip comes. As it is I am quite at a loss. Whom am I to marry? I think I have scarcely seen a single man with whom such a union would be possible since I left London. Doubtless there are men whom, if I chose to encourage, I might marry. But no matrimonial lot is even remotely offered me which seems to me truly desirable. And even if that were the case there would be many obstacles. The least allusion to such a thing is most offensive to Papa. An article entitled "Currer Bell" has lately appeared in *The Palladium*, a new periodical published in Edinburgh. It is an eloquent production, and one of such warm sympathy and high appreciation as I had never expected to see. It makes mistakes about authorship, &c, but those I hope one day to set right. Mr. X—— (the little man) first informed me of this article. I was somewhat surprised to receive his letter, having concluded nine months ago that there would be no more correspondence from that quarter. I enclose a note from him received subsequently, in answer to my acknowledgment. Read it, and tell me exactly how it impresses you regarding the writer's character, &c. He is deficient neither in spirit nor sense.

October 14th, 1850.

I return Q——'s letter. She seems quite happy and fully satisfied of her husband's affection. Is this the usual way of spending the honeymoon? To me it seems as if they overdo it. That travelling, and tugging, and fagging about, and getting drenched and muddled, by no means harmonises with my notions of happiness. Besides, the two meals a day, &c, would do one up. It all reminds me too sharply of the few days I spent with V—— in London nearly ten years since, when I was many a time fit to drop with the fever and the faintness resulting from long fasting and excessive fatigue. However, no doubt a bride can bear such things better than others. I smiled to myself at some passages. She has wondrous faith in her husband's intellectual powers and acquirements. V——'s illusions will soon be over, but Q——'s will not—and therein she is happier than he.... I suppose —— will probably discover that he, too, wants a wife. But I will say no more. You know I disapprove of jesting and teasing on these matters. Idle words sometimes do unintentional harm.

December, 1850.

I got home all right yesterday soon after two o'clock, and found Papa, thank God, well and free from cold. To-day some amount of sickliness and headache is bothering me, but nothing to signify.... The Christmas books waiting for me were, as I expected, from Thackeray, Mrs.

Gaskell, and Mr. Ruskin. No letter from Mr. W——. It is six weeks since I heard from him. I feel uneasy, but do not like to write. *The Examiner* is very sore about my Preface, because I did not make it a special exception in speaking of the mass of critics. The soreness is unfortunate and gratuitous, for in my mind I certainly excepted it. Another paper shows painful sensitiveness on the same account; but it does not matter, these things are all transitory.

The "Preface" to which she alludes in the foregoing letter, was that to her collected edition of Emily and Anne Brontë's works, in which she makes allusion to the fact that the "critics failed to do justice" to "Wuthering Heights" and "Agnes Grey" when they were published.

Jan. 20th, 1851.

Thank you heartily for the two letters I owe you. You seem very gay at present, and provided you only take care not to catch cold with coming home at night, I am not sorry to hear it; a little movement, cheerfulness, stimulus, is not only beneficial, but necessary. Your last letter but one made me smile. I think you draw great conclusions from small inferences. I think those "fixed intentions" you fancy are imaginary. I think the "under-current" amounts simply to this, a kind of natural liking and sense of something congenial. Were there no vast barrier of age, fortune, &c, there is perhaps enough personal regard to make things possible which now are impossible. If men and women married because they like each other's temper, look, conversation, nature, and so on—and if, besides, years were more nearly equal—the chance you allude to might be admitted as a chance; but other reasons regulate matrimony—reasons of convenience, of connection, of money. Meantime I am content to know him as a friend, and pray God to continue to me the common sense to look on one so young, so rising, and so hopeful in no other light. The hint about the Rhine disturbs me; I am not made of stone and what is mere excitement to others is fever to me. However it is a matter for the future, and long to look forward to. As I see it now, the journey is out of the question—for many reasons—I rather wonder he should think of it. Good-bye. Heaven grant us both some quiet wisdom and strength, not merely to bear the trial of pain, but to resist the lure of pleasure when it comes in such a shape as our better judgment disapproves.

Feb. 26th, 1851.

You ought always to conclude that when I don't write it is simply because I have nothing particular to say. Be sure that ill news will travel fast enough, and good news too when such commodity comes. If I could often *be* or *seem* in brisk spirits, I might write oftener, knowing that my letters would amuse. But as times go, a glimpse of sunshine now and then is as much as one has a right to expect. However, I get on very decently. I am now and then tempted to break through my resolution of not having you to come before summer, and to ask you to come to this Patmos in a week or two. But it would be dull—very dull—for you…. What would you say to coming here the week after next to stay only just so long as you could comfortably bear the monotony? If the weather were dry, and the moors fine, I should not mind it so much—we could walk for change.

About this time it is clear that Miss Brontë was suffering from one of her periodical attacks of nervous exhaustion. She makes repeated references in her letters to her ailments, attributing them generally to her liver, and she also mentions frequently an occurrence which had given her not a little anxiety and concern. This was an offer of marriage from a business man in a good position, whom she had already met in London. The following letters, which are inserted here without regard to the precise date, and of which Mrs. Gaskell has merely used half-a-dozen lines, relate to this subject:

> You are to say no more about "Jupiter" and "Venus." What do you mean by such heathen trash? The fact is no fallacy can be wilder, and I won't have it hinted at, even in jest because my common sense laughs it to scorn. The idea of X—— shocks me less; it would be a more likely match, if "matches" were at all in question, *which they are not*. He still sends his little newspaper, and the other day there came a letter of a bulk, volume, pith, judgment, and knowledge, worthy to have been the product of a giant.
>
> X—— has been, and is gone; things are just as they were. I only know, in addition to the slight information I possessed before, that this Australian undertaking is necessary to the continued prosperity of his firm, that he alone was pronounced to possess the power and means to carry it out successfully, that mercantile honour, combined with his own sense of duty, obliged him to accept the post of honour and of danger to which he has been appointed, that he goes with great personal reluctance, and that he contemplates an absence of five years. He looked much thinner and older. I saw him very near, and once through my glass. The resemblance to Branwell struck me forcibly; it is marked. He is not ugly, but very peculiar. The lines in his face show an inflexibility, and, I must add, a hardness of character, which does not attract. As he stood near me, as he looked at me in his keen way, it was all I could do to stand my ground tranquilly and steadily, and not to recoil

as before. It is no use saying anything if I am not candid. I avow then that on this occasion, predisposed as I was to regard him very favourably, his manners and his personal appearance scarcely pleased me more than at the first interview. He gave me a book at parting, requesting in his brief way that I would keep it for his sake, and adding hastily: "I shall hope to hear from you in Australia; your letters *have* been and *will* be a greater refreshment than you can think or I can tell." And so he is gone, and stern and abrupt little man as he is, too often jarring as are his manners, his absence and the exclusion of his idea from my mind, leave me certainly with less support and in deeper solitude than before. You see, dear Nell, we are still precisely on the same level. *You*are not isolated. I feel that there is a certain mystery about this transaction yet, and whether it will ever be cleared up to me, I do not know. However, my plain duty is to wean my mind from the subject, and if possible to avoid pondering over it.... I feel that in his way he has a regard for me; a regard which I cannot bring myself entirely to reciprocate in kind, and yet its withdrawal leaves a painful blank. I have just got your note. Above, you have all the account of my visitor. I dare not aver that your kind wish that the visit would yield me more pleasure than pain has been fulfilled. Something at my heart aches and gnaws drearily. But I must cultivate fortitude.

Thank you for your kind note. It was kind of you to write it, though it *was* your school-day. I never knew you to let a slight impediment stand in your way when doing a friendly action. Certainly I shall not soon forget last Friday, and never, I think, the evening and night succeeding that morning and afternoon. Evils seldom come singly, and soon after X—— was gone Papa grew much worse. He went to bed early. Was sick and ill for an hour, and when at last he began to doze and I left him, I came down to the dining-room with a sense of weight, fear, and desolation hard to express and harder to endure. A wish that you were with me did cross my mind; but I repelled it as a most selfish wish. Indeed it was only short-lived; my natural tendency in moments of this sort is to get through the struggle alone; to think that one is burdening others makes all worse. You speak to me in soft, consolatory accents; but I hold far sterner language to myself, dear Nell. An absence of five years; a dividing expanse of three oceans; the wide difference between a man's active career and a woman's passive existence. These things are almost equivalent to a life-long separation. But there is another thing which forms a barrier more difficult to pass than any of these. Would X—— and I ever suit? Could I ever feel for him enough love to accept of him as a husband? Friendship, gratitude, esteem, I have; but each moment that he came near me, and that I could see his eyes fastened upon me, my veins ran ice. Now that he is away I feel far more gently towards him; it is only close by that I grow rigid. I did not want to be proud nor intend to be proud, but I was forced to be so. Most true is it that we are overruled by One above us, that in His hands our very will is as clay in the hands of the potter.

I trust Papa is not worse; but he varies. He has never been down to breakfast but once since you left. The circumstance of having him to think about just now is good for me in one way; it keeps my thoughts off other matters which have been complete bitterness and ashes; for I do assure you a more entire crumbling away of a seeming foundation of support and prospect of hope than that which I allude to can scarcely be realised.

I have heard from X—— to-day, a quiet little note. He returned to London a week since on Saturday. He leaves England next month. His note concludes with asking whether he has any chance of seeing me in London before that time. I must tell him that I have already fixed June for my visit, and, therefore, in all human probability we shall see each other no more. There is still a want of plain mutual understanding in this business, and there is sadness and pain in more ways than one. My conscience, I can truly say, does not *now* accuse me of having treated X—— with injustice or unkindness. What I once did wrong in this way I have endeavoured to remedy both to himself and in speaking of him to others. I am sure he has estimable and sterling qualities; but with every disposition—with every wish—with every intention even to look on him in the most favourable point of view at his last visit, it was impossible for me in my inmost heart to think of him as one that might one day be acceptable as a husband.... No, if X—— be the only husband fate offers to me, single I must always remain. But yet at times I grieve for him; and perhaps it is superfluous, for I cannot think he will suffer much—a hard nature, occupation, change of scene will befriend him.

I have had a long, kind letter from Miss Martineau lately. She says she is well and happy. Also I have had a very long letter from Mr. ——, the first for many weeks. He speaks of X—— with much respect and regret, and says he will be greatly missed by many friends. I discover with some surprise that Papa has taken a decided liking to X——. The marked kindness of his manner to him when he bade him good-bye, exhorting him to be "true to himself, his country, and his God," and wishing him all good wishes, struck me with some astonishment at the time; and whenever he has alluded to him since, it has been with significant eulogy.... You say Papa has penetration. On this subject I believe he has indeed. I have told him nothing, yet he seems to be *au fait* to the whole business. I could think at some moments his guesses go further than mine. I believe he thinks a prospective union, deferred for five years, with such a decorous, reliable personage, would be a very proper and advisable affair. However I ask no questions, and he asks me none; and if he did I should have nothing to tell him.

The summer following this affair of the heart witnessed another visit to London, where she heard Mr. Thackeray's lectures on the humourists. How she enjoyed listening to her idol, in one of his best moods, need not be told. Some there are still living who remember that first lecture, when all London had assembled to listen to the author of "Vanity Fair," and the rumour suddenly ran round the room that the author of "Jane Eyre" was among the audience. Men and women were at fault at first, in their efforts to distinguish "Currer Bell" in that brilliant company of literary and social notabilities; but at last she was discovered hiding under the motherly wing of a chaperon, timid, blushing, but excited and pleased—*not* at the attention she herself attracted, but at the treat she had in prospect. One or two gentlemen sought and obtained introductions to her—amongst them Lord Carlisle and Mr. Monckton Milnes. They were not particularly impressed by the appearance or the speech of the parson's daughter. Her person was insignificant, her dress somewhat rustic, her language quaintly precise and formal, her manner odd and constrained. Altogether this was a woman whom even London could not lionise; somebody outwardly altogether too plain, simple, unpretending, to admit of hero-worship. Within there was, as we know, something entirely exceptional and extraordinary; but, like Lucy Snowe, she still kept her real self hidden under a veil which no casual friend or chance acquaintance was allowed to lift. It was but a brief visit to the "Big Babylon," and then back to

Haworth, to loneliness and duty! In July, 1851, she writes from the parsonage to one of her friends as follows:

> My first feeling on receiving your note was one of disappointment, but a little consideration sufficed to show me that "all was for the best." In truth it was a great piece of extravagance on my part to ask you and Ellen together; it is much better to divide such good things. To have your visit in prospect will console me when hers is in retrospect. Not that I mean to yield to the weakness of clinging dependently to the society of friends, however dear; but still as an occasional treat I must value and even seek such society as a necessary of life. Let me know then whenever it suits your convenience to come to Haworth, and, unless some change I cannot now foresee occurs, a ready and warm welcome will await you. Should there be any cause rendering it desirable to defer the visit, I will tell you frankly. The pleasures of society I cannot offer you; nor those of fine scenery. But I place very much at your command—the moors, some books, a series of quiet "curling-hair-times," and an old pupil into the bargain. Ellen may have told you that I spent a month in London this summer. When you come you shall ask what questions you like on that point, and I will answer to the best of my stammering ability. Do not press me much on the subject of the Crystal Palace. I went there five times, and certainly saw some interesting things, and the *coup d'œil* is striking and bewildering enough. But I never was able to get up any raptures on the subject, and each renewed visit was made under coercion rather than my own free will. It is an excessively bustling place; and after all, its wonders appeal too exclusively to the eye, and rarely touch the heart or head. I make an exception to the last assertion in favour of those who possess a large range of scientific knowledge. Once I went with Sir David

Brewster, and perceived that he looked on objects with other eyes than mine.

X.

"VILLETTE."

With the autumn of 1851 another epoch in the life of Charlotte Brontë was ushered in. She began to write "Villette." Something has already been said of the true character of that marvellous book, in which her own deepest experiences and ripest wisdom are given to the world. Of the manner in which it was written her readers know nothing. Yet this, the best-beloved child of her genius, was brought forth with a travail so bitter that more than once she was tempted to lay aside her pen and hush her voice for ever. Every sentence was wrung from her as though it had been a drop of blood, and the book was built up bit by bit, amid paroxysms of positive anguish, occasioned in part by her own physical weakness and suffering, but still more by the torture through which her mind passed as she depicted scene after scene from the darkest chapter in her own life, for the benefit of those for whom she wrote. It is from her letters that at this time also we get the best indications of what she was passing through. Few, perhaps, reading these letters would suppose that their writer was at that very time engaged in the production of a great masterpiece, destined to hold its own among the ripest and finest fruits of English genius. But no one can read them without seeing how true the woman's soul was, how deep her sympathy with those she loved, how keen her criticisms of even the dull and commonplace characters around her, how vivid and sincere her interest in everything which was passing either in the great world which lay afar off, or in the little world the drama of which was being enacted under her own eyes. Even the ordinary incidents mentioned in her letters, the chance expressions which drop from her pen, have an interest when we remember who it is that speaks, and at what hour in her life this speech falls from her.

September, 1851.

I have mislaid your last letter, and so cannot look it over to see what there is in it to answer; but it is time it was answered in some fashion, whether I have anything to say or not. Miss ——'s note is very like her. All that talk about "friendship," "mutual friends," "auld lang syne," &c., sounds very like palaver. Mrs. —— wrote to me a week or a fortnight since—a well-meaning, amiable note, dwelling a good deal, excusably perhaps, on the good time that is coming. I mean, to speak plain English, on her expectation of soon becoming a mother. No doubt it is very natural in her to feel as if no woman had ever been a mother before; but I could not help inditing an answer calculated to shake her up a bit. A day or two since I had another note from her, quite as good as usual, but I think a trifle nonplussed by the rather unceremonious fashion in which her terrors and the expected personage were handled.... It is useless to tell you how I live. I endure life; but whether I enjoy it or not is another question. However, I get on. The weather, I think, has not been very good lately; or else the beneficial effects of change of air and scene are evaporating. In spite of regular exercise the old headaches and starting, wakeful nights are coming upon me again. But I *do* get on, and have neither wish nor right to complain.

October, 1851.

I am not at all intending to go from home at present. I have just refused successively, Miss Martineau, Mrs. Gaskell, and Mrs. Forster. I could not go if I would. One person after another in the house has been ailing for the last month and more. First Tabby had the influenza, then Martha took it and is ill in bed now, and I grieve to say Papa too has taken cold. So far I keep pretty well, and am thankful for it, for who else would nurse them all? Some painful mental worry I have gone through this autumn; but there is no use in dwelling on all that. At present I seem to have some respite. I feel more disinclined than ever for letter-writing.... Life is a struggle.

November, 1851.

Papa, Tabby, and Martha are at present all better, but yet none of them well. Martha especially looks feeble. I wish she had a better constitution. As it is, one is always afraid of giving her too much to do; and yet there are many things I cannot undertake myself; and we do not like to change when we have had her so long. The other day I received the enclosed letter from Australia. I had had one before from the same quarter, which is still unanswered. I told you I did not expect to hear thence—nor did I. The letter is long, but it will be worth your while to read it. In its way it has merit—that cannot be denied—abundance of information, talent of a certain kind, alloyed (I think) here and there with errors of taste. This little man with all his long letters remains as much a conundrum to me as ever. Your account of the H—— "domestic joys" amused me much. The good folks seem very happy; long may they continue so! It somewhat cheers me to know that such happiness *does* exist on earth.

November, 1851.

All here is pretty much as usual.... The only events of my life consist in that little change occasional letters bring. I have had two from Miss W—— since she left Haworth, which touched me much. She seems to think so much of a little congenial company, a little attention and kindness. She says she has not for many days known such enjoyment as she experienced during the ten days she stayed here. Yet you know what Haworth is—dull enough. Before answering X——'s letter from Australia I got up my courage to write to —— and beg him to give me an impartial account of X——'s character and disposition, owning that I was very much in the dark on these points and did not like to continue correspondence without further information. I got the answer which I enclose. Since receiving it I have replied to X—— in a calm, civil manner. At the earliest I cannot hear from him again before the spring.

December, 1851.

I hope you have got on this last week well. It has been very trying here. Papa so far has borne it unhurt; but these winds and changes have given me a bad cold; however, I am better now than I was. Poor old Keeper (Emily's dog) died last Monday morning, after being ill one night. He went gently to sleep; we laid his old faithful head in the garden. Flossy is dull, and misses him. There was something very sad in losing the old dog; yet I am glad he met a natural fate. People kept hinting that he ought to be put away, which neither Papa nor I liked to think of. If I were near a town, and could get cod-liver oil fresh and sweet, I really would most gladly take your advice and try it; but how I could possibly procure it at Haworth I do not see.... You ask about "The Lily and the Bee." If you have read it, you have effected an exploit beyond me. I glanced at a few pages, and laid it down hopeless, nor can I now find courage to resume it. But then, I never liked Warren's writings. "Margaret Maitland" is a good book, I doubt not.

At this point the illness of which she makes light in these letters increased to such an extent as to alarm her father, and at last she consented to lay aside her work and allow herself the pleasure and comfort of a visit from her friend. The visit was a source of happiness whilst it lasted; but when it was over the depression returned, and there was a serious relapse. Something of her sufferings at this time—whilst "Villette" was still upon the stocks—will be gathered from the following letter, dated January 1852:

I wish you could have seen the coolness with which I captured your letter on its way to Papa, and at once conjecturing its tenor, made the contents my own. Be quiet. Be tranquil. It is, dear Nell, my decided intention to come to B—— for a few days when I *can* come; but of this last I must positively judge for myself, and I must take my time. I am better to-day—much better; but you can have little idea of the sort of condition into which mercury throws people to ask me to go from home anywhere in close or open carriage. And as to talking—four days ago I could not well have articulated three sentences. Yet I did not need nursing, and I kept out of bed. It was enough to burden myself; it would have been misery to me to have annoyed another.

March, 1852.

The news of E. T.'s death came to me last week in a letter from M——, a long letter, which wrung my heart so in its simple, strong, truthful emotion, I have only ventured to read it once. It ripped up half-scarred wounds with terrible force—the death-bed was just the same—breath failing, &c. She fears she will now in her dreary solitude become "a stern, harsh, selfish woman." This fear struck home. Again and again I have felt it for myself; and what is *my* position to M——'s? I should break out in energetic wishes that she would return to England, if reason would permit me to believe that prosperity and happiness would there await her. But I see no such prospect. May God help her as God only can help!

To another friend she writes as follows, in reply to an invitation to leave Haworth for a short visit:

March 12th, 1852.

Your kind note holds out a strong temptation, but one that *must be resisted*. From home I must not go unless health or some cause equally imperative render a change necessary. For nearly four months now (*i.e.* since I first became ill) I have not put pen to paper; my work has been lying untouched, and my faculties have been rusting for want of exercise; further relaxation is out of the question, and *I will not permit myself to think of it*. My publisher groans over my long delays; I am sometimes provoked to check the expression of his impatience with short and crusty answers. Yet the pleasure I now deny myself I would fain regard as only deferred. I heard something about your purposing to visit Scarborough in the course of the summer; and could I by the close of July or August bring my task to a certain point, how glad should I be to join you there for a while!... However, I dare not lay plans at this distance of time; for me so much must depend, first, on Papa's health (which throughout the winter has been, I am thankful to say, really excellent), and, second, on the progress of work—a matter not wholly contingent on wish or will, but lying in a great measure beyond the reach of effort, or out of the pale of calculation.

As the summer advanced her sufferings were scarcely abated, and at last, in search of some relief, she made a sudden visit by herself to Filey, inspired in part by her desire to see the memorial-stone erected above her sister's grave at Scarborough.

Filey Bay, June, 1852.

My dear Miss ——,—Your kind and welcome note reached me at this place, where I have been staying three weeks *quite alone*. Change and sea-air had become necessary. Distance and other considerations forbade my accompanying Ellen to the South, much as I should have liked it had I felt quite free and unfettered. Ellen told me some time ago that you were not likely to visit Scarborough till the autumn, so I forthwith packed my trunk and betook myself here. The first week or ten days I greatly feared the seaside would not suit me, for I suffered almost incessantly from headache and other harassing ailments; the weather, too, was dark, stormy, and excessively—*bitterly*—cold. My solitude under such circumstances partook of the character of desolation; I had some dreary evening hours and night vigils. However, that passed. I think I am now better and stronger for the change, and in a day or two hope to return home. Ellen told me that Mr. W—— said people with my tendency to congestion of the liver should walk three or four hours every day; accordingly, I have walked as much as I could since I came here, and look almost as sunburnt and weather-beaten as a fisherman or a bathing-woman, with being out in the open air. As to my work, it has stood obstinately still for a long while; certainly a torpid liver makes a torpid brain. No spirit moves me. If this state of things does not entirely change, my chance of a holiday in the autumn is not worth much; yet I should be very sorry not to meet you for a little while at Scarborough. The duty to be discharged at Scarborough was the chief motive that drew me to the east coast. I have been there, visited the churchyard, and seen the stone. There were five errors; consequently I had to give directions for its being re-faced and re-lettered.

The sea-air did her good; but she was still unable to carry her great work forward, in spite of the urgent pressure put upon her by those who in this respect merely expressed the impatience of the public.

Haworth, July, 1852.

I am again at home, where (thank God) I found all well. I certainly feel much better than I did, and would fain trust that the improvement may prove permanent.... The first fortnight I was at Filey I had constantly recurring pain in the right side, and sick headache into the bargain. My spirits at the same time were cruelly depressed—prostrated sometimes. I feared the miseries and the suffering of last winter were all returning; consequently I am now indeed thankful to find myself so much better.... You ask about Australia. Let us dismiss the subject in a few words, and not recur to it. All is silent as the grave.

Cornhill is silent too; there has been bitter disappointment there at my having no work ready for this season. Ellen, we must not rely upon our fellow-creatures—only on ourselves, and on Him who is above both us and them. My *labours*, as you call them, stand in abeyance, and I cannot hurry them. I must take my own time, however long that time may be.

August, 1852.

I am thankful to say that Papa's convalescence seems now to be quite confirmed. There is scarcely any remainder of the inflammation in his eyes, and his general health progresses satisfactorily. He begins even to look forward to resuming his duty ere long, but caution must be observed on that head. Martha has been very willing and helpful during Papa's illness. Poor Tabby is ill herself at present with English cholera, which complaint, together with influenza, has lately been almost universally prevalent in this district. Of the last I have myself had a touch; but it went off very gently on the whole, affecting my chest and liver less than any cold has done for the last three years.... I write to you about yourself rather under constraint and in the dark; for your letters, dear Nell, are most remarkably oracular, dropping nothing but hints which tie my tongue a good deal. What, for instance, can I say to your last postscript? It is quite sibylline. I can hardly guess what checks you in writing to me. Perhaps you think that as *I* generally write with some reserve, you ought to do the same. *My* reserve, however, has its origin not in design, but in necessity. I am silent because I have literally *nothing to say*. I might, indeed, repeat over and over again that my life is a pale blank, and often a very weary burden, and that the future sometimes appals me; but what end could be answered by such repetition, except to weary you and enervate myself? The evils that now and then wring a groan from my heart lie in my position—not that I am a *single* woman and likely to remain a *single* woman, but because I am a lonely woman and likely to be *lonely*. But it cannot be helped, and therefore *imperatively must be borne*, and borne, too, with as few words about it as may be. I write this just to prove to you that whatever you would freely *say* to me you may just as freely write. Understand that I remain just as resolved as ever not to allow myself the holiday of a visit from you till *I* have done my work. After labour, pleasure; but while work was lying at the wall undone, I never yet could enjoy recreation.

Haworth Augst 25th /52

Dear Ellen

I am thankful to say that Papa's convalescence seems now to be quite confirmed. There is scarcely any household lately been almost universally prevalent in this district, of the last I have just myself had a touch — but it went off very gently on the whole — affecting my chest and liver less than any cold has done for the last three years.

I trust, dear Ellen, you are well in health yourself — this visit to the South has not so far been productive of unmingled pleasure — yet it may bring you future benefit in more ways than one.

I write to you about yourself rather under constraint — and in the dark — for your letters, dear Nell — are most remarkably oracular — dropping nothing but hints — which tie my tongue a good deal. What for instance can I say to your last letter? It is quite sibylline. I can hardly guess what checks you in writing to me — there is certainly no one in this house towards or slanders to whom I should shew your notes — and I do not imagine they are in any peril in passing through the Post-Office

SIMILE LETTER OF CHARLOTTE BRONTË.

Slowly page after page of "Villette" was now being written. The reader sees from these letters that the book was composed in no happy mood. Writing to her publisher a few weeks after the date of the last letter printed above, she says: "I can hardly tell you how I hunger to hear some opinions beside my own, and how I have sometimes desponded and almost despaired, because there was no one to whom to read a line, or of whom to ask a counsel. 'Jane Eyre' was not written under such circumstances, nor were two-thirds of 'Shirley.' I got so miserable about it that I could bear no allusion to the book. It is not finished yet; but now I hope." But though her work pressed so incessantly upon her, and her feverish anxiety to have it done weighed so heavily upon her health and spirits, she could still find time to answer her friend's letters in a way which showed that her interest in the outer world was as keen as ever:

September, 1852.

Thank you for A——'s notes. I like to read them, they are so full of news, but they are illegible. A great many words I really cannot make out. It is pleasing to hear that M—— is doing so well, and the tidings about —— seem also good. I get a note from —— every now and then, but I fear my last reply has not given much satisfaction. It contained a taste of that unpalatable commodity called *advice*—such advice, too, as might be, and I dare say was, construed into faint reproof. I can scarcely tell what there is about —— that, in spite of one's conviction of her amiability, in spite of one's sincere wish for her welfare, palls upon one, satiates, stirs impatience. She *will* complacently put forth opinions and tastes as her own which are *not* her own, nor in any sense natural to her. My patience can really hardly sustain the test of such a jay in borrowed plumes. She prated so much about the fine wilful spirit of her child, whom she describes as a hard, brown little thing, who will do nothing but what pleases himself, that

I hit out at last—not very hard, but enough to make her think herself ill-used, I doubt not. Can't help it. She often says she is not "absorbed in self," but the fact is, I have seldom seen anyone more unconsciously, thoroughly, and often weakly egotistic. Then, too, she is inconsistent. In the same breath she boasts her matrimonial happiness and whines for sympathy. Don't understand it. With a paragon of a husband and child, why that whining, craving note? Either her lot is not all she professes it to be, or she is hard to content.

In October the resolute determination to allow herself no relaxation until "Villette" was finished broke down. She was compelled to call for help, and to acknowledge herself beaten in her attempt to crush out the yearning for company:

October, 1852.

Papa expresses so strong a wish that I should ask you to come, and I feel some little refreshment so absolutely necessary myself, that I really must beg you to come to Haworth for one single week. I thought I would persist in denying myself till I had done my work, but I find it won't do. The matter refuses to progress, and this excessive solitude presses too heavily. So let me see your dear face, Nell, just for one reviving week. Could you come on Wednesday? Write to-morrow, and let me know by what train you would reach Keighley, that I may send for you.

The visit was a pleasant one in spite of the weariness of body and mind which troubled Charlotte. She laid aside her task for that "one little week," went out upon the moors with her friend, talked as of old, and at last, when she was left alone once more, declared that the change had done her "inexpressible good." Writing to her friend immediately after the latter had left her, she says:

> Your note came only this morning. I had expected it yesterday, and was beginning actually to feel weary—like you. This won't do. I am afraid of caring for you too much. You must have come upon —— at an unfavourable moment, seen it under a cloud. Surely they are not always or often thus, or else married life is indeed but a slipshod paradise. I only send *The Examiner*, not having yet read *The Leader*. I was spared the remorse I feared. On Saturday I fell to business, and as the welcome mood is still decently existent, and my eyes consequently excessively tired with scribbling, you must excuse a mere scrawl. Papa was glad to hear you had got home well—as well as we.... I do miss my dear bed-fellow; no more of that calm sleep.

Her pen now began to move more quickly, and the closing chapters of "Villette" were written with comparative ease, so that at last she writes thus, on November 22nd:

> Monday morning.
>
> Truly thankful am I to be able to tell you that I finished my long task on Saturday, packed and sent off the parcel to Cornhill. I said my prayers when I had done it. Whether it is well or ill done I don't know. D. V., I will now try to wait the issue quietly. The book, I think, will not be considered pretentious, nor is it of a character to excite hostility. As Papa is pretty well, I may, I trust, dear Nell, do as you wish me, and come for a few days to B——. Miss Martineau has also urgently asked me to go and see her. I promised, if all were well, to do so at the close of November or the commencement of December, so that I could go on from B—— to Westmoreland. Would Wednesday suit you? "Esmond" shall come with me—*i.e.* Thackeray's novel.

Every reader knows in what fashion "Villette" ends, and most persons also know from Mrs. Gaskell that the reason why the actual issue is left in some uncertainty was the author's filial desire to gratify her father. Charlotte herself was firmly resolved that she would *not* make Lucy Snowe the happy wife of Paul Emanuel. She never meant to "appoint her lot in pleasant places." Lucy was to bear the storm and stress of life in the same manner as that in which her creator had been compelled to bear it; and she was to be left in the end alone, robbed for ever of the hope of spending the happy afternoon of her existence in the sunshine of love and congenial society. But Mr. Brontë, altogether unconscious of that tragedy of heart-sickness and soul-weariness which was being enacted under his own roof, and which furnished so striking a parallel to the story which ran through "Villette," would not brook a gloomy ending to the tale, and by protestations and entreaties induced his daughter at least so far to alter her plan as to leave the issue in doubt.

So "Villette" went its way, as "Jane Eyre" and "Shirley " had done before it, from the secluded parsonage at Haworth up to the busy publishing-house in Cornhill, and thence out into the world. There was some fear on Charlotte's part when the MS. had been despatched. She herself was gradually forming that which remained the fixed conviction of her life—the conviction that in "Villette" she had done her best, and that, for good or for ill, by it her reputation must stand or fall. But she was intensely anxious, as we have seen, to have the opinions of others upon the story. Nor was it only a general verdict on its merits for which she called. She was uneasy upon some minor points. According to her wont, she had taken most of her characters from life, and it was not during her stay at Brussels alone that she had studied the models which she employed when writing the book. Naturally, she was curious to know whether she had painted her portraits too literally. So "Villette" was allowed to pass, whilst still in MS., into the hands of the original of "Dr. John." When that gentleman had read the story, and criticised all the characters with the freedom of unconsciousness, her mind was set at rest, and she knew that she had not transgressed the bounds which divide the story-teller from the biographer.

In the meantime, her work done, she hurried away from Haworth to spend a well-earned holiday at B—— with her friend. "Esmond" accompanied her, and the quiet afternoons were spent in reading it aloud. On December 9th she writes from Haworth, announcing her safe return to her own home:

> I got home safely at five o'clock yesterday afternoon, and, I am most thankful to say, found Papa and all the rest quite well. I did my business satisfactorily in Leeds, getting the head-dress rearranged as I wished. It is now a very different matter to the bushy, tasteless thing it was before. On my arrival I found no proof-sheets, but a letter from Mr. S——, which I would have enclosed, but so many words are scarce legible you would have no pleasure in reading it. He continues to make a mystery of his "reason"; something in the third volume sticks confoundedly in his throat; and as to the "female character" about which I asked, he responds that "she is an odd, fascinating little puss," but affirms that "he is not in love with her." He tells me also that he will answer no more questions about "Villette." This morning I have a brief note from Mr. Williams, intimating that he has not yet been permitted to read the third volume. Also there is a note from Mrs. ——, very kind. I almost wish I could still look on that kindness just as I used to do: it was very pleasant to me once. Write *immediately*, dear Nell, and tell me how your mother is. Give my kindest regards to her and all others at B——. Everybody seemed very good to me this last visit. I remember it with corresponding pleasure.

The private reception of "Villette" was not altogether that for which its author had hoped. Her publisher had objections to urge against certain features of the story, and those who saw the book in manuscript were not slow to express their own disapproval. It was evident that there was disappointment at Cornhill; and the proud spirit of Miss Brontë was keenly troubled. The letters in which she dwells on what was passing at that time need not be reproduced here, for their purport is sufficiently indicated by that which has just been given. But it is worth while to notice the scrupulous modesty with which she listened to all that was said by those who found fault, her careful anxiety to understand their objections, such as they were, and her perfect readiness to discuss every point raised with them. Of irritability under this criticism there is no trace, only a certain sadness and sorrow at the discovery that she had not succeeded in impressing others as she had hoped to do. Yet she is scarcely surprised that it is so. Had she not written years before, when "Shirley" was first produced, these words?—

> No matter, whether known or unknown, misjudged or the contrary, I am resolved not to write otherwise. I shall bend as my powers tend. The two human beings who understood me, and whom I understood, are gone. I have some that love me yet, and whom I love without expecting, or having a right to expect, that they shall perfectly understand me. I am satisfied, but I must have my own way in the matter of writing.... I am thankful to God who gave me the faculty; and it is for me a part of my religion to defend this gift and to profit by its possession.

So now she is not astonished at finding herself misunderstood. Nor is she angry. She is perfectly ready to explain her real meaning to those who have misjudged her, but she is resolute in abiding by what she has written. The work wrung from her during those two years of pain and sorrow is not work which can be altered at will to please another. Even to meet the entreaties of her father she had refused to do more than draw a veil over the catastrophe in which the plot ends; and she cannot introduce new incidents, or lay on new colours, because the little circle of critics sitting in judgment on her manuscript have pronounced it to be imperfect. "I fear they" (the readers) "must be satisfied with what is offered. My palette affords no brighter tints; were I to attempt to deepen the reds or burnish the yellows, I should but blotch." Yet she admits that those who judge the book only from the outside have some reason to complain that it is not as other novels are:

> You say that Lucy Snowe may be thought morbid and weak, unless the history of her life be more freely given. I consider that she *is* both morbid and weak at times; her character sets up no pretensions to unmixed strength, and anybody living her life would necessarily become morbid. It was no impetus of healthy feeling which urged her to the confessional, for instance; it was the semi-delirium of solitary grief and sickness. If, however, the book does not express all this, there must be a great fault somewhere. I might explain away a few other points, but it would be too much like drawing a picture and then writing underneath the name of the object intended to be represented.

Happily, the heart of the great reading world is bigger and truer as a whole than any part of it is. What those who read the manuscript of "Villette" failed to see at the first glance was seen instantly by the public when the book was placed in its hands. From critics of every school and degree there came up a cry of wonder and admiration, as men saw out of what simple characters and commonplace incidents genius had evoked this striking work of literary art. Popular, perhaps, the book could scarcely hope to be, in the vulgar acceptation of the word. The author had carefully avoided the "flowery and inviting" course of romance, and had written in silent obedience to the stern dictates of an inspiration which, as we have seen, only came at intervals, leaving her between its visits cruelly depressed and pained, but which when it came held her spell-bound and docile. Yet out of the dull record of humble woes, marked by no startling episodes, adorned by few of the flowers of poetry, she had created such a heart-history as remains to this day without a rival in the school of English fiction to which it belongs.

I bring together a batch of notes, not all addressed to the same person, which give her account of the reception and success of the book:

February 11th, 1853.

Excuse a very brief note, for I have time only to thank you for your last kind and welcome letter, and to say that, in obedience to your wishes, I send you by this day's post two reviews—*The Examiner* and *The Morning Advertiser*—which, perhaps, you will kindly return at your leisure. Ellen has a third—*The Literary Gazette*—which she will likewise send. The reception of the book has been favourable thus far—for which I am thankful—less, I trust, on my own account than for the sake of those few real friends who take so sincere an interest in my welfare as to be happy in my happiness.

February 15th.

I am very glad to hear that you got home all right, and that you managed to execute your commissions in Leeds so satisfactorily. You do not say whether you remembered to order the Bishop's dessert; I shall know, however, by to-morrow morning. I got a budget of no less than seven papers yesterday and to-day. The import of all the notices is such as to make my heart swell with thankfulness to

Him who takes note both of suffering and work and motives. Papa is pleased too. As to friends in general, I believe I can love them still without expecting them to take any large share in this sort of gratification. The longer I live, the more plainly I see that gentle must be the strain on fragile human nature. It will not bear much.

I have heard from Mrs. Gaskell. Very kind, panegyrical, and so on. Mr. S—— tells me he has ascertained that Miss Martineau *did* write the notice in *The Daily News*. J. T. offers to give me a regular blowing-up and setting down for £5, but I tell him *The Times* will probably let me have the same gratis.

March 10th, 1853.

I only got *The Guardian* newspaper yesterday morning, and have not yet seen either *The Critic* or *Sharpe's Magazine*. *The Guardian* does not wound me much. I see the motive, which, indeed, there is no attempt to disguise. Still I think it a choice little morsel for foes (Mr. —— was the first to bring the news of the review to Papa), and a still choicer morsel for "friends" who—bless them!—while they would not perhaps positively do one an injury, still take a dear delight in dashing with bitterness the too sweet cup of success. Is *Sharpe's* small article like a bit of sugar-candy, too, Ellen? or has it the proper wholesome wormwood flavour? Of course I guess it will be like *The Guardian*. My "dear friends" will weary of waiting for *The Times*. "O Sisera! why tarry the wheels of thy chariot so long?"

March 22nd.

Thank you for sending ——'s notes. Though I have not attended to them lately, they always amuse me. I like to read them; one gets from them a clear enough idea of her sort of life. ——'s attempts to improve his good partner's mind make me smile. I think it all right enough, and doubt not they are happy in their way; only the direction he gives his efforts seems of rather problematic wisdom. Algebra and optics! Why not enlarge her views by a little well-chosen general reading? However, they do right to amuse themselves in their own way. The rather dark view you seem to take of the general opinion about "Villette" surprises me the less, as only the more unfavourable reviews seem to have come in your way. Some reports reach me of a different tendency; but no matter; time will show. As to the character of Lucy Snowe, my intention from the first was that she should not occupy the pedestal to which "Jane Eyre" was raised by some injudicious admirers. She is where I meant her to be, and where no charge of self-laudation can touch her.

XI.

MARRIAGE AND DEATH.

Every book, as we know, has its secret history, hidden from the world which reads only the printed pages, but legible enough to the author, who sees something more than the words he has set down for the public to read. Thackeray tells us how, reading again one of his smaller stories, written at a sad period of his own life, he brought back all the scene amid which the little tale was composed, and woke again to a consciousness of the pangs which tore his heart when his pen was busy with the imaginary fortunes of the puppets he had placed upon the mimic stage. Between the lines he read quite a different story from that which was laid before the reader. I have tried to show how largely this was the case with Charlotte Brontë's novels. Each was a double romance, having one meaning for the world, and another for the author. Yet she herself, when she wrote "Shirley" and "Villette," had no conception of the strange blending of the secret currents of the two books which was in store for her, or of the unexpected fate which was to befall the real heroine of her last work—to wit, herself.

I have told how fixed was her belief that "Lucy Snowe's" fate was to be a tragic one—a life the closing years of which were to be spent in loneliness and anguish, and amid the bitterness of withered hopes. Very few readers can have forgotten the closing passage of "Villette," in which the catastrophe, though veiled, can be readily discovered:

The sun passes the equinox; the days shorten, the leaves grow sere; but—he is coming.

Frosts appear at night; November has sent his fogs in advance; the wind takes its autumn moan; but—he is coming.

The skies hang full and dark—a rack sails from the west; the clouds cast themselves into strange forms—arches and broad radiations; there rise resplendent mornings—glorious, royal, purple as a monarch in his state; the heavens are one flame; so wild are they, they rival battle at its thickest—so bloody, they shame Victory in her pride. I know some signs of the sky; I have noted them ever since childhood. God, watch that sail! Oh! guard it!

The wind shifts to the west. Peace, peace, Banshee—"keening" at every window! It will rise—it will swell—it shrieks out long: wander as I may through the house this night, I cannot lull the blast. The advancing hours make it strong: by midnight, all sleepless watchers hear and fear a wild south-west storm....

Peace, be still! Oh! a thousand weepers, praying in agony on waiting shores, listened for that voice, but it was not uttered—not uttered till, when the hush came, some could not feel it; till, when the sun returned, his light was night to some!

In darkness such as here is shadowed forth, Charlotte Brontë believed that her own life would close; all sunshine gone, all joys swept clean away by the bitter blast of death, all hopes withered or uprooted. But the end which she pictured was not to be. God was more merciful than her own imaginings; and at eventide there was light and peace upon her troubled path.

Those who turn to the closing passage of "Shirley" will find there reference to "a true Christian gentleman," who had taken the place of the hypocrite Malone, one of the famous three curates of the story. This gentleman, a Mr. McCarthy, was, like the rest, no fictitious personage. His original was to be found in the person of Mr. Nicholls, who for several years had lived a simple, unobtrusive life at Haworth, as curate to Mr. Brontë, and whose name often occurs in Charlotte's letters to her friend. In none of these references to him is there the slightest indication that he was more than an honoured friend. Nor was it so. Whilst Mr. Nicholls, dwelling near Miss Brontë, and observing her far more closely than any other person could do, had formed a deep and abiding attachment for her, she herself was wholly unconscious of the fact. Its first revelation came upon her as something like a shock; as something also like a reproach. Whilst she had thought herself alone, doomed to a life of solitude and pain, a tender yet a manly love had all the while been growing round her.

It is obvious that the letters which she addressed at this time (December, 1852) to her friend cannot be printed here. Yet no letters more honourable to the woman, the daughter, and the lover have ever been penned. There is no restraint now in the outpourings of her heart. Her friend is taken into her full confidence, and every hope and fear and joy is spoken out as only women who are pure and truthful and entirely noble can venture to speak out. Mrs. Gaskell has briefly but distinctly stated the broad features of this strange love story, giving such promise at the time, so happy and beautiful in its brief fruition, so soon to be quenched in the great darkness. Mr. Brontë resented the attentions of Mr. Nicholls to his daughter in a manner which brought to light all the sternness and bitterness of his character. There had been of late years a certain mellowing of his disposition, which Charlotte had dwelt upon with hopeful joy, as her one comfort in her lonely life at Haworth. How much he owed to her none knew but himself. When he was sinking under the burden of his son's death, she had rescued him; when, for one dark and bitter interval, he had sought refuge from grief and remorse in the coward's solace, her brave heart, her gentleness, her unyielding courage, had brought him back again from evil ways, and sustained and kept him in the path of honour; and now his own ambitions were more than satisfied by her success; he found himself shining in the reflected glory of his daughter's fame, and sunned himself, poor man, in the light and warmth. But all the old jealousy, the intense acerbity of his character, broke out when he saw another person step between himself and her, and that other no idol of the great world of London, but simply the honest man who had dwelt almost under his own roof-tree for years.

When, having heard with surprise and emotion, the story of Mr. Nicholls's attachment, Charlotte communicated his offer to her father, "agitation and anger disproportionate to the occasion ensued. My blood boiled with a sense of injustice. But Papa worked himself into a state not to be trifled with. The veins on his forehead started up like whipcord, and his eyes became suddenly bloodshot. I made haste to promise that on the morrow Mr. Nicholls should have a distinct refusal." It so happened that very soon after this, that is to say when "Villette" was published, Miss Martineau caused deep pain to its writer by condemning the manner in which "all the female characters in all their thoughts and lives" were represented as "being full of one thing—love." The critic not unjustly pointed out that love was not the be-all and the end-all of a woman's life. Perhaps her pen would not have been so sharp in touching on this subject, had she known with what quiet self-sacrifice the author of "Villette" had but a few weeks before set aside her own preferences and inclinations, and submitted her lot to her father's angry will. This truly must be reckoned as another illustration of the extent to which the *Quarterly* reviewer of 1848 had formed an accurate conception of the character of "Currer Bell."

Not only was the struggle which followed sharp and painful, it was also stubborn and prolonged. Mr. Nicholls resigned the curacy he had held so many years, and prepared to leave Haworth. Mr. Brontë not only showed no signs of relenting, but openly exulted in his departure, and lost no opportunity of expressing in bitterly sarcastic language his opinion of his colleague's conduct. How deeply Charlotte suffered at this time is proved by the letters before me. Firmly convinced that her first duty was to the parent whose only remaining stay she was, she never wavered in her determination to sacrifice every wish of her own to his comfort. But her heart was racked with pity for the man who was suffering through his love for her, and her indignation was roused to fever-heat by the gross injustice of her father's conduct.

> Compassion or relenting is no more to be looked for from Papa than sap from firewood. I never saw a battle more sternly fought with the feelings than Mr. N. fights with his, and when he yields momentarily, you are almost sickened by the sense of the strain upon him. However, he is to go, and I cannot speak to him or look at him or comfort him a whit—and I must submit. Providence is over all; that is the only consolation.
>
> In all this—she says, after speaking again of the severity of the struggle—it is not *I* who am to be pitied at all, and of course nobody pities me. They all think in Haworth that I have disdainfully refused him. If pity would do him any good he ought to have, and I believe has, it. They may abuse me if they will. Whether they do or not I can't tell.
>
> I thought of you on New Year's Day, and hope you got well over your formidable tea-making. I am busy, too, in my little way, preparing to go to London this week—a matter which necessitates some little application to the needle. I find it quite necessary I should go to superintend the press, as Mr. S—— seems quite determined not to let the printing get on till I come. I have actually only received three proof-sheets since I was at Brookroyd. Papa wants me to go too, to be out of the way, I suppose; but I am sorry for one other person whom nobody pities but me.... They don't understand the nature of his feelings, but I

see now what they are. Mr. N—— is one of those who attach themselves to very few, whose sensations are close and deep, like an underground stream, running strong but in a narrow channel. He continues restless and ill. He carefully performs the occasional duty, but does not come near the church, procuring a substitute every Sunday. A few days since he wrote to Papa requesting permission to withdraw his resignation. Papa answered that he should only do so on condition of giving his written promise never again to broach the obnoxious subject either to him or to me. This he has evaded doing, so the matter remains unsettled. I feel persuaded the termination will be, his departure for Australia. Dear Nell, without loving him, I don't like to think of him suffering in solitude, and wish him anywhere so that he were happier. He and Papa have never met or spoken yet.

During this crisis in her life, when suffering had come to her in a new and sharp form, but when happily the black cloud was lit up on the other side by the rays of the sun, she went up to London to spend a few weeks. From the letters written during her visit I make these extracts:

January 11th, 1853.

I came here last Wednesday. I had a delightful day for my journey, and was kindly received at the close. My time has passed pleasantly enough since I came, yet I have not much to tell you; nor is it likely I shall have. I do not mean to go out much or see many people. Sir J. S—— wrote to me two or three times before I left home, and made me promise to let him know when I should be in town, but I reserve to myself the right of deferring the communication till the latter part of my stay. All in this house appear to be pretty much as usual, and yet I see some changes. Mrs. —— and her daughter look well enough; but on Mr. —— hard work is telling early. Both his complexion, his countenance, and the very lines of his features are altered. It is rather the remembrance of what he was than the fact of what he is which can warrant the picture I have been accustomed to give of him. One feels pained to see a physical alteration of this kind; yet I feel glad and thankful that it is *merely* physical. As far as I can judge, mind and manners have undergone no deterioration—rather, I think, the contrary.

January 19th, 1853.

I still continue to get on very comfortably and quietly in London, in the way I like, seeing rather things than persons. Being allowed to have my own choice of sights this time I selected the *real* rather than the *decorative* side of life. I have been over two prisons, ancient and modern, Newgate and Pentonville; also the Bank, the Exchange, the Foundling Hospital; and to-day, if all be well, I go with Dr. Forbes to see Bethlehem Hospital. Mrs. —— and her daughters are, I believe, a little amazed at my gloomy tastes; but I take no notice. Papa, I am glad to say, continues well. I enclose portions of two notes of his which will show you better than anything I can say how he treats a certain subject. My book is to appear at the close of this month. Mrs. Gaskell wrote to beg that it should not clash with "Ruth," and it was impossible to refuse to defer the publication a week or two.

The visit to London did good; but it could not remove the pain which she suffered during this period of conflict.

Haworth, May 19th, 1853.

It is almost a relief to hear that you only think of staying at G—— a month; though of course one must not be selfish in wishing you to come home soon.... I cannot help feeling satisfaction in finding that the people here are getting up a subscription to offer a testimonial of respect to Mr. N—— on his leaving the place. Many are expressing both their commiseration and esteem for him. The churchwardens recently put the question to him plainly: Why was he going? Was it Mr. Brontë's fault or his own? His own, he answered. Did he blame Mr. Brontë? No, he did not: if anybody was wrong, it was himself. Was he willing to go? No; it gave him great pain. Yet he is not always right. I must be just. Papa addressed him at the school tea-drinking with *constrained* civility, but still with *civility*. He did not reply civilly; he cut short further words. This sort of treatment is what Papa never will forget or forgive. It inspires him with a silent bitterness not to be expressed.... It is a dismal state of things. The weather is fine now, dear Nell. We will take these sunny days as a good omen for your visit.

May 27th, 1853.

You will want to know about the leave-taking. The whole matter is but a painful subject, but I must treat it briefly. The testimonial was presented in a public meeting. Mr. F—— and Mr. G—— were there. Papa was not very well, and I advised him to stay away, which he did. As to the last Sunday, it was a cruel struggle. Mr. N—— ought not to have had to take any duty. He left Haworth this morning at six o'clock. Yesterday evening he called to render into Papa's hands the deeds of the National School, and to say good-bye. They were busy cleaning, washing the paint, &c., so he did not find me there. I would not go into the parlour to speak to him in Papa's presence. He went out, thinking he was not to see me; and indeed till the very last moment I thought it best not. But perceiving that he stayed long before going out at the gate, and remembering his long grief, I took courage, and went out, trembling and miserable. I found him leaning against the garden door.... Of course I went straight to him. Very few words were interchanged; those few barely articulate: several things I should have liked to ask him were swept entirely from my memory. Poor fellow! but he wanted such hope and such encouragement as I *could* not give him. Still I trust he must know now that I am not cruelly blind and indifferent to his constancy and grief. For a few weeks he goes to the South of England—afterwards he takes a curacy somewhere in Yorkshire, but I don't know where. Papa has been far from strong lately. I dare not mention Mr. N——'s name to him. He speaks of him quietly and without opprobrium to others; but to me he is implacable on the matter. However, he is gone—gone—and there's an end of it! I see no chance of hearing a word about him in future, unless some stray shred of intelligence comes through Mr. G—— or some other second-hand source.

The remainder of the year 1853 was a chequered one. Mr. Nicholls left Haworth; Charlotte remained with her father. Those who saw her at this time bear testimony to the unfailing, never-flagging devotion she displayed towards one who was wounding her cruelly. But she bore this sorrow, like those which had preceded it, bravely and cheerfully. To her friend she opened her heart at times, revealing something of what she was suffering; but to all others she was silent.

Haworth, April 13th, 1853.

My dear Miss ——,—Your last kind letter ought to have been answered long since, and would have been, did I find it practicable to proportion the promptitude of the response to the value I place upon my correspondents and their communications. You will easily understand, however, that the contrary rule often holds good, and that the epistle which importunes often takes precedence of that which interests. My publishers express entire satisfaction with the reception which has been accorded to "Villette." And, indeed, the majority of the reviews has been favourable enough. You will be aware, however, that there is a minority, small in character, which views the work with no favourable eye. "Currer Bell's" remarks on Romanism have drawn down on him the condign displeasure of the High Church party, which displeasure has been unequivocally expressed through their principal organs, *The Guardian*, *The English Churchman*, and *The Christian Remembrancer*. I can well understand that some of the charges launched against me by these publications will tell heavily to my prejudice in the minds of most readers. But this must be borne; and for my part, I can suffer no accusation to oppress me much which is not supported by the inward evidence of Conscience and Reason. "Extremes meet," says the proverb; in proof whereof I would mention that Miss Martineau finds with "Villette" nearly the same fault as the Puseyites. She accuses me of attacking Popery "with virulence," of going out of my way to assault it "passionately." In other respects she has shown, with reference to the work, a spirit so strangely and unexpectedly acrimonious, that I have gathered courage to tell her that the gulf of mutual difference between her and me is so wide and deep, the bridge of union so slight and uncertain, I have come to the conclusion that frequent intercourse would be most perilous and unadvisable, and have begged to adjourn *sine die* my long-projected visit to her. Of course she is now very angry, but it cannot be helped. Two or three weeks since I received a long and kind letter from Mr. ——, which I answered a short time ago. I believe he thinks me a much better advocate for *change*, and what is called "political progress," than I am. However, in my reply I did not touch on these subjects. He intimated a wish to publish some of his own MSS. I fear he would hardly like the somewhat dissuasive tendency of my answer; but really, in these days of headlong competition, it is a great risk to publish.

April 18th, 1853.

If all be well, I think of going to Manchester about the close of this week. I only intend staying a few days; but I can say nothing about coming back by B——. Do not expect me; I would rather see you at Haworth by-and-by. Two or three weeks since, Miss Martineau wrote to ask why she did not hear from me, and to press me to go to Ambleside. Explanations ensued; the notes on each side were quite civil; but, having deliberately formed my resolution on substantial grounds, I adhered to it. I have declined being her visitor, and bid her good-bye. It is best so; the antagonism of our natures and principles was too serious to be trifled with.

This difference with Miss Martineau is not a thing to dwell on now. The pity is that two women so truthful, so sincere, so bold in their utterances should ever have differed. Charlotte Brontë had known how to stand bravely by Miss Martineau when she believed that the latter was suffering because of her honestly-formed opinions; she had known how to speak on her behalf with timely generosity and force. But her sensitive nature was wounded to the quick by criticisms which she believed to be unjust; and so these two great women parted, and met again no more.

To the mental pain which she was now suffering from her father's conduct there was added keen physical torture. During this summer of 1853 many of her letters contain sentences like this: "I have been suffering most severely for ten days with continued pain in the head—on the nerves it is said to be. Blistering at last seems to have done it some good; but I am yet weak and bewildered." A visit from Mrs. Gaskell, who came to see how Haworth looked in its autumn robe of splendour, did her some good; but still more was gained by a journey to the seaside in the company of her old friend and schoolmistress, Miss Wooler, before which she had addressed to her the following letter:

Haworth, August 30th, 1853.

My dear Miss W.,—I was from home when your kind letter came, and, as it was not forwarded, I did not get it till my return. All the summer I have felt the wish and cherished the intention to join you for a brief period at the seaside; nor do I yet entirely relinquish the purpose, though its fulfilment must depend on my father's health. At present he complains so much of weakness and depressed spirits, that no thoughts of leaving him can be entertained. Should he improve, however, I would fain come to you before autumn is quite gone.

My late absence was but for a week, when I accompanied Mr. and Mrs. —— and baby on a trip to Scotland. They went with the intention of taking up their quarters at Kirkcudbright, or some watering-place on the Solway Firth. We hardly reached that locality, and had stayed but one night, when the baby (that rather despotic member of modern households) exhibited some symptoms of indisposition. To my unskilled perception its ailments appeared very slight, nowise interfering with its appetite or spirits; but parental eyes saw the matter in a different light. The air of Scotland was pronounced unpropitious to the child, and consequently we had to retrace our steps. I own I felt some little reluctance to leave "bonnie Scotland" so soon and so abruptly, but of course I could not say a word, since, however strong on my own mind the impression that the ailment in question was very trivial and temporary (an impression confirmed by the issue), I could not be absolutely certain that such was the case; and had any evil consequences followed a prolonged stay, I should never have forgiven myself.

Ilkley was the next place thought of. We went there, but I only remained three days, for, in the hurry of changing trains at one of the stations, my box was lost, and without clothes I could not stay. I have heard of it twice, but have not yet regained it. In all probability it is now lying at Kirkcudbright, where it was directed.

Notwithstanding some minor trials, I greatly enjoyed this little excursion. The scenery through which we travelled from Dumfries to Kirkcudbright (a distance of thirty miles, performed outside a stage-coach) was beautiful, though not at all of a peculiarly Scottish character, being richly cultivated and well wooded. I liked Ilkley, too, exceedingly, and shall long to revisit the place. On the whole, I thought it for the best that circumstances obliged me to return home so soon, for I found Papa far from well. He is something better now, yet I shall not feel it right to leave him again till I see a more thorough re-establishment of health and strength.

With some things to regret and smile at, I saw things to admire in the small family party with which I travelled. Mr. —— makes a most devoted father and husband.

I admired his great kindness to his wife; but I rather groaned (inwardly) over the unbounded indulgence of both parents towards their only child. The world does not revolve round the sun; that is a mistake. Certain babies, I plainly perceive, are the important centre of all things. The papa and mamma could only take their meals, rest, and exercise at such times and in such manner as the despotic infant permitted. While Mrs. —— eat her dinner, Mr. —— relieved guard as nurse. A nominal nurse, indeed, accompanied the party, but her place was a sort of anxious waiting sinecure, as the child did not fancy her attendance. Tenderness to offspring is a virtue, yet I think I have seen mothers who were most tender and thoughtful, yet in very love for their children would not permit them to become tyrants either over themselves or others.

I shall be glad and grateful, my dear Miss W., to hear from you again whenever you have time or inclination to write—though, as I told you before, there is no fear of my misunderstanding silence. Should you leave Hornsea before winter sets in, I trust you will just come straight to Haworth, and pay your long-anticipated visit there before you go elsewhere. Papa and the servants send their respects. I always duly deliver your kind messages of remembrance, because they give pleasure.

December came, and she writes to this friend expressing her wonder as to how she is spending the long winter evenings—"alone, probably, like me." It was a dreary winter for her; but the spring was at hand. Mr. Brontë, studying his daughter with keen eyes, could not hide from himself the fact that her health and spirits were drooping now as they had never drooped before. All work with the pen was laid aside; and household cares, attendance upon her father or on the old servant, who now also needed to be waited upon, occupied her time; but her heart was heavy with a burden such as she had never previously known. At last the stern nature of the man was broken down by his genuine affection for his daughter. His opposition to her marriage was suddenly laid aside; he asked her to recall Mr. Nicholls to Haworth, and with characteristic waywardness he now became as anxious that the wedding should take place as he had ever been that it should be prevented.

There was a curious misadventure regarding the letter inviting Mr. Nicholls to Haworth, which is explained in the first of the letters I now quote.

Haworth, March 28th, 1854.

The enclosure in yours of yesterday puzzled me at first, for I did not immediately recognise my own handwriting. When I did, the sensation was one of consternation and vexation, as the letter ought by all means to have gone on Friday. It was intended to relieve him from great anxiety. However, I trust he will get it to-day; and, on the whole, when I think it over, I can only be thankful that the mistake was no worse, and did not throw the letter into the hands of some indifferent and unscrupulous person. I wrote it after some days of indisposition and uneasiness, and when I felt weak and unfit to write. While writing to *him* I was at the same time intending to answer *your* note; which I suppose accounts for the confusion of ideas shown in the mixed and blundering address.

I wish you could come about Easter rather than at another time, for this reason. Mr. Nicholls, if not prevented, proposes coming over then. I suppose he will be staying at Mr. ——'s, as he has done two or three times before; but he will be frequently coming here, which would enliven your visits a little. Perhaps, too, he might take a walk with us occasionally. Altogether, it would be a little change for you, such as you know I could not always offer. If all be well, he will come under different circumstances to any that have attended his visits before. Were it otherwise, I should not ask you to meet him, for when aspects are gloomy and unpropitious, the fewer there are to suffer from the cloud, the better. He was here in January, and was then received.... I trust it will be a little different now. Papa has breakfasted in bed to-day, and has not yet risen. His bronchitis is still troublesome. I had a bad week last week, but am greatly better now, for my mind is a little relieved, though very sedate, and rising only to expectations the most moderate. Some time, perhaps in May, I may be in your neighbourhood, and shall then hope to come to B.; but, as you will understand from what I have now stated, I could not come before. Think it over, dear E., and come to Haworth if you can.

April 11th, 1854.

The result of Mr. Nicholls's visit is that Papa's consent is gained and his respect won, for Mr. Nicholls has in all things proved himself disinterested and forbearing. He has shown, too, that, while his feelings are exquisitely keen, he can freely forgive.... In fact, dear Ellen, I am engaged. Mr. Nicholls in the course of a few months will return to the curacy of Haworth. I stipulated that I would not leave Papa, and to Papa himself I proposed a plan of residence which should maintain his seclusion and convenience uninvaded, and in a pecuniary sense bring him gain instead of loss. What seemed at one time impossible is now arranged, and Papa begins really to take a pleasure in the prospect. For myself, dear E——, while thankful to One who seems to have guided me through much difficulty, much and deep distress and perplexity of mind, I am still very calm.... What I taste of happiness is of the soberest order. Providence offers me this destiny. Doubtless, then, it is the best for me; nor do I shrink from wishing those dear to me one not less happy. It is possible that our marriage may take place in the course of the summer. Mr. Nicholls wishes it to be in July. He spoke of you with great kindness, and said he hoped you would be at our wedding. I said I thought of having no other bridesmaid. Did I say right? I mean the marriage to be literally *as quiet as possible.* Do not mention these things as yet. Good-bye. There is a strange, half-sad feeling in making these announcements. The whole thing is something other than the imagination paints it beforehand—cares, fears, come mixed inextricably with hopes. I trust yet to talk the matter over with you.

So at length the day had dawned, and every letter now is filled with the hopes and cares of the expectant bride.

April 15th.

I hope to see you somewhere about the second week in May. The Manchester visit is still hanging over my head; I have deferred it and deferred it, but have finally promised to go about the beginning of next month. I shall only stay about three days; then I spend two or three days at H., then come to B. The three visits must be compressed into the space of a fortnight, if possible. I suppose I shall have to go to Leeds. My purchases cannot be either expensive or extensive. You must just resolve in your head the bonnets and dresses: something that can be turned to decent use and worn after the wedding-day will be best, I think. I wrote immediately to Miss W——, and received a truly kind letter from her this morning. Papa's mind seems wholly changed about this matter; and he has said, both to me and when I was not there, how much happier he feels since he allowed all to be settled. It is a wonderful relief for me to hear him treat the thing rationally, and quietly and amicably to talk over with him themes on which once I dared not touch. He is rather anxious that things should get forward now, and takes quite an interest in the arrangement of preliminaries. His health improves daily, though this east wind still keeps up a slight irritation in the throat and chest. The feeling which has been disappointed in Papa was *ambition*—paternal pride—ever a restless feeling, as we all know. Now that this unquiet spirit is exorcised, justice, which was once quite forgotten, is once more listened to, and affection, I hope, resumes some power. My hope is that in the end this arrangement will turn out more truly to Papa's advantage than any other it was in my power to achieve. Mr. N. only in his last letter refers touchingly to his earnest desire to prove his gratitude to Papa by offering support and consolation to his declining age. This will not be mere *talk* with him. He is no talker, no dealer in mere professions.

April 28th.

Papa, thank God! continues to improve much. He preached twice on Sunday, and again on Wednesday, and was not tired. His mind and mood are different to what they were; so much more cheerful and quiet. I trust the illusions of ambition are quite dissipated, and that he really sees it is better to relieve a suffering and faithful heart, to secure in its fidelity a solid good, than unfeelingly to abandon one who is truly attached to *his* interests as well as mine, and pursue some vain empty shadow.

Hemsworth, May 6th.

I came here on Thursday afternoon. I shall stay over Saturday and Sunday, and, if all be well, I hope to come to B. on Monday, after dinner, and just in time for tea. I leave you to judge by your own feelings whether I long to see you or not. —— tells me you are looking better. She tells me also that I am not—rather ugly, as usual. But never mind that, dear Nell—as, indeed, you never did. On the whole, I *feel* very decently at present, and within the last fortnight have had much respite from headache. You are kind in being so much in earnest in wishing for Mr. N. to come to B., and I am sorry that circumstances do not favour such a step. But, knowing how matters stood, I did not repeat the proposal to him, for I thought it would be like tempting him to forget duty.

In the following letters, in addition to the pleasing side-lights which they throw upon her life in its new aspect, there is another feature which deserves to be noticed—that is, the exceeding tenderness with which the writer watches over her friend. The new love entering into her heart has but made the old love stronger, and she lavishes upon the sole remaining companion of her youth the care and affection which can no longer be bestowed upon sisters of her own blood.

Haworth, May 14th.

I took the time of the Leeds, Keighley, Skipton trains from the February time-table, and when I got to Leeds found myself all wrong. The trains on that line were changed. One had that moment left the station—indeed, it was just steaming away; there was not another till a quarter after five o'clock; so I had just four hours to sit and twirl my thumbs. I got over the time somehow, but

I was vexed to think how much more pleasantly I might have spent it at B. It was just seven o'clock when I reached home. I found Papa well. It seems he has been particularly well during my absence, but to-day he is a little sickly, and only preached once. However, he is better again this evening. I could not leave you, dear Ellen, with a very quiet mind, or take away a satisfied feeling about you. Not that I think that bad cough lodged in a dangerous quarter; but it shakes your system, wears you out, and makes you look ill. *Take care of it, do, dear Ellen. Avoid the evening air for a time*; keep in the house when the weather is cold. Observe these precautions till the cough is quite gone, and you regain strength, and feel better able to bear chill and change. Believe me, it does not suit you at present to be much exposed to variations of temperature. I send the mantle with this, but have made up my mind not to let you have the cushion now, lest you should sit stitching over it too closely. It will do any time, and whenever it comes will be your present all the same.

May 22nd.

I wonder how you are, and whether that harassing cough is better; but I am afraid the variable weather of last week will not have been favourable to improvement. I *will* not and *do* not believe the cough lies on any vital organ. Still it is a mark of weakness, and a warning to be scrupulously careful about undue exposure. Just now, dear Ellen, an hour's inadvertence might derange your whole constitution for years to come—might throw you into a state of chronic ill-health which would waste, fade, and wither you up prematurely. So, once and again, TAKE CARE. If you go to ——, or any other evening party, pack yourself in blankets and a feather-bed to come home, also fold your boa twice over your mouth, to serve as a respirator. Since I came home I have been very busy sketching. The little new room is got into order now, and the green and white curtains are up. They exactly suit the papering, and look neat and clean enough. I had a letter a day or two since, announcing that Mr. N. comes to-morrow. I feel anxious about him, more anxious on one point than I dare quite express to myself. It seems he has again been suffering sharply from his rheumatic affection. I hear this not from himself, but from another quarter. He was ill whilst I was at Manchester and B. He uttered no complaint to me, dropped no hint on the subject. Alas! he was hoping he had got the better of it; and I know how this contradiction of his hopes will sadden him. For unselfish reasons he did so earnestly wish this complaint might not become chronic. I fear—I fear—but, however, I mean to stand by him now, whether in weal or woe. This liability to rheumatic pain was one of the strong arguments used against the marriage. It did not weigh, somehow. If he is doomed to suffer, it seems that so much the more will he need care and help. And yet the ultimate possibilities of such a case are appalling. Well, come what may, God help and strengthen both him and me. I look forward to to-morrow with a mixture of impatience and anxiety. Poor fellow! I want to see with my own eyes how he is.

Haworth, June 7th.

I am very glad and thankful to hear that you continue better, though I am afraid your cough will have returned a little during the late chilly change in the weather. Are you taking proper care of yourself, and either staying in the house or going out warmly clad, and with a boa doing duty as a respirator? On this last point I incline particularly to insist, for you seemed careless about it, and unconscious how much atmospheric harm the fine thick hairs of the fur might ward off. I was very miserable about Papa again some days ago. While the weather was so sultry and electric, about a week since, he was suddenly attacked with deafness, and complained of other symptoms which showed the old tendency to the head. His spirits, too, became excessively depressed. It was all I could do to keep him up, and I own I was sad and depressed myself. However he took some medicine, which did him good. The change to cooler weather, too, has suited him. The temporary deafness has quite disappeared for the present, and his head is again clear and cool. I can only earnestly trust he will continue better. That unlucky —— continues his efforts to give what trouble he can, and I am obliged to conceal things from Papa's knowledge as well as I can, to spare him that anxiety which hurts him so much.... I feel compelled to throw the burden of the contest upon Mr. Nicholls, who is younger and can bear it better. The worst of it is, Mr. N. has not Papa's right to speak and act, or he would do it to purpose. I should then have to mediate, not rouse; to play the part of

Feather-bed 'twixt castle-wall
And heavy brunt of cannon-ball.

June 16th.

My dear Miss W——,—Owing to certain untoward proceedings, matters have hitherto been kept in such a state of uncertainty that I could not make any approach towards fixing the day; and now, if I would avoid inconveniencing Papa, I must hurry. I believe the commencement of July is the furthest date upon which I can calculate; possibly I may be obliged to accept one still nearer—the close of June. I cannot quite decide till next week. Meantime, will you, my dear Miss W——, come as soon as you possibly can, and let me know at your earliest convenience the day of your arrival. I have written to Ellen, begging her to communicate with you..... Your absence would be a real and grievous disappointment. Papa also seems much to wish your presence. Mr. Nicholls enters with true kindness into my wish to have all done quietly; and he has made such arrangements as will, I trust, secure literal privacy. Yourself, Ellen, and Mr. S. will be the only persons present at the ceremony. Mr. and Mrs. G. are asked to the breakfast afterwards. I know you will kindly excuse this brief note, for I am and have been *very* busy, and must still be busy up to the very day. Give my sincere love to all Mr. C——'s family. I hope Mr. C. and Mr. Nicholls may meet some day. I believe mutual acquaintance would in time bring mutual respect; but one of them, at least, requires *knowing* to be*appreciated*. And I must say that I have not yet found him to lose with closer knowledge. I make no grand discoveries, but I occasionally come upon a quiet little nook of character which excites esteem. He is always reliable, truthful, faithful, affectionate; a little unbending, perhaps, but still persuadable and open to kind influence—a man never, indeed, to be driven, but who may be led.

HAWORTH CHURCH.

The marriage took place on June 29th, 1854. A neighbouring clergyman read the service; Charlotte's "dear Nell" was the solitary bridesmaid; her old schoolmistress, whose friendship had ever been dear to her, Miss Wooler, gave her away; and visitors to Haworth who are shown the marriage register will see that these two faithful and trusted friends were the only witnesses. Immediately after the marriage the bride and bridegroom started for Ireland, to visit some of the relatives of Mr. Nicholls. "I trust I feel thankful to God for having enabled me to make a right choice; and I pray to be enabled to repay as I ought the affectionate devotion of a truthful, honourable, unboastful man," are words which appear in the first letter written from Ireland. A month later the bride writes as follows to her friend:

Dublin, July 28th, 1854.

I really cannot rest any longer without writing you a line, which I have literally not had time to do during the last fortnight. We have been travelling about, with only just such cessation as enabled me to answer a few of the many notes of congratulation forwarded, and which I dared not suffer to accumulate till my return, when I know I shall be busy enough. We have been to Killarney, Glen Gariffe, Tarbert, Tralee, Cork, and are now once more in Dublin again on our way home, where we hope to arrive next week. I shall make no effort to describe the scenery through which we have passed. Some parts have exceeded all I ever imagined. Of course, much pleasure has sprung from all this, and more, perhaps, from the kind and ceaseless protection which has ever surrounded me, and made travelling a different matter to me from what it has heretofore been. Dear Nell, it is written that there shall be no unmixed happiness in this world. Papa has not been well, and I have been longing, *longing intensely* sometimes, to be at home. Indeed, I could enjoy and rest no more, and so home we are going.

It was a new life to which she was returning. Wedded to one who had proved by years of faithfulness and patience how strong and real was his love for her, it seemed as though peace and sunshine, the brightness of affection and the pleasures of home, were at length about to settle upon her and around her. The bare sitting-room in the parsonage, which for six years of loneliness and anguish had been peopled only by the heart-sick woman and the memories of those who had left her, once more resounded with the voices of the living. The husband's strong and upright nature furnished something for the wife to lean against; the painful sense of isolation which had so long oppressed her vanished utterly, and in its place came that "sweet sense of depending" which is the most blessed fruit of a trustful love. A great calm seemed to be breathed over the spirit of her life after the fitful fever which had raged so long; and her friends saw new shoots of tenderness, new blossoms of gentleness and affection, peeping forth in nooks of her character which had hitherto been barren. Of her letters during these happy months of peace and expectation I cannot quote much; they are too closely intertwined with the life of those who survive to permit of this being done; but all of them breathe the same spirit. They show that the courage, the patience, the cheerfulness with which the rude buffetings of fate had been borne in that stormy middle-passage of her history, had brought their own reward; and that joy had come at last, not perhaps in the shape she had imagined in her early youth, but as a substantial reality, and no longer a mocking illusion.

August 9th, 1854.

—— will probably end by accepting ——; and judging from what you say, it seems to me that it would be rational to do so. If, indeed, some one else whom she preferred *wished* to have her, and had duly and sincerely come forward, matters would be different. But this it appears is not the case; and to cherish any *unguarded* and unsustained preference is neither right nor wise. Since I came home I have not had one unemployed moment. My life is changed indeed; to be wanted continually, to be constantly called for and occupied, seems so strange; yet it is a marvellously good thing. As yet I don't quite understand how some wives grow so selfish. As far as my experience of matrimony goes, I think it tends to draw you out and away from yourself.... Dear Nell, during the last six weeks the colour of my thoughts is a good deal changed. I know more of the realities of life than I once did. I think many false ideas are propagated, perhaps unintentionally. I think those married women who indiscriminately urge their acquaintance to marry, much to blame. For my part I can only say with deeper sincerity and fuller significance, what I always said in theory: Wait God's will. Indeed, indeed, Nell, it is a solemn and strange and perilous thing for a woman to become a wife. Man's lot is far, far different.... Have I told you how much better Mr. Nicholls is? He looks quite strong and hale. To see this improvement in him has been a great source of happiness to me; and, to speak truth, a source of wonder too.

Haworth, September 7th, 1854.

I send a French paper to-day. You would almost think I had given them up, it is so long since one was despatched. The fact is they had accumulated to quite a pile during my absence. I wished to look them over before sending them off, and as yet I have scarcely found time. That same *time* is an article of which I once had a large stock always on hand; where it is all gone to now it would be difficult to say, but my moments are very fully occupied. Take warning, Ellen. The married woman can call but a very small portion of each day her own. Not that I complain of this sort of monopoly as yet, and I hope I never shall incline to regard it as a misfortune, but it certainly exists. We were both disappointed that you could not come on the day I mentioned. I have grudged this splendid weather very much. The moors are in their glory; I never saw them fuller of purple bloom; I wanted you to see them at their best. They are fast turning now, and in another week, I fear, will be faded and sere. As soon as ever you can leave home, be sure to write and let me know.... Papa continues greatly better. My husband flourishes; he begins indeed to express some slight alarm at the growing improvement in his condition. I think I am decent—better certainly than I was two months ago; but people don't compliment me as they do Arthur—excuse the name; it has grown natural to use it now.

Haworth, September 16th, 1854.

My dear Miss ——,—You kindly tell me not to write while Ellen is with me; I am expecting her this week; and as I think it would be wrong long to defer answering a letter like yours, I will reduce to practice the maxim: "There is no time like the present," and do it at once. It grieves me that you should have had any anxiety about my health; the cough left me before I quitted Ireland, and since my return home I have scarcely had an ailment, except occasional headaches. My dear father, too, continues much better. Dr. B—— was here on Sunday, preaching a sermon for the Jews, and he gratified me much by saying that he thought Papa not at all altered since he saw him last—nearly a year ago. I am afraid this opinion is rather flattering; but still it gave me pleasure, for I had feared that he looked undeniably thinner and older. You ask what visitors we have had. A good many amongst the clergy, &c., in the neighbourhood, but none of note from a distance. Haworth is, as you say, a very quiet place; it is also difficult of access, and unless under the stimulus of necessity, or that of strong curiosity, or finally, that of true and tried friendship, few take courage to penetrate to so remote a nook. Besides, now that I am married, I do not expect to be an object of much general interest. Ladies who have won some prominence (call it either *notoriety* or celebrity) in their single life, often fall quite into the background when they change their names.

But if true domestic happiness replace fame, the change is indeed for the better. Yes, I am thankful to say that my husband is in improved health and spirits. It makes me content and grateful to hear him, from time to time, avow his happiness in the brief but plain phrase of sincerity. My own life is more occupied than it used to be; I have not so much time for thinking: I am obliged to be more practical, for my dear Arthur is a very practical as well as a very punctual, methodical man. Every morning he is in the national school by nine o'clock; he gives the children religious instruction till half-past ten. Almost every afternoon he pays visits amongst the poor parishioners. Of course he often finds a little work for his wife to do, and I hope she is not sorry to help him. I believe it is not bad for me that his bent should be so wholly towards matters of real life and active usefulness—so little inclined to the literary and contemplative. As to his continued affection and kind attentions, it does not become me to say much of them; but as yet they neither change nor diminish. I wish, my dear Miss ——, *you* had some kind, faithful companion to enliven your solitude at R——, some friend to whom to communicate your pleasure in the scenery, the fine weather, the pleasant walks. You never complain, never murmur, never seem otherwise than thankful; but I know you must miss a privilege none could more keenly appreciate than yourself.

There are other letters like the foregoing, all speaking of the constant occupation of time, which once hung heavily, all giving evidence that peace and love had made their home in her heart, all free from that strain of sadness which was so common in other years. One only of these letters, that written on the morrow of her last Christmas Day, need be quoted, however.

Haworth, December 26th.

I return Mrs. ——'s letter: it is as you say, very genuine, truthful, affectionate, *maternal*, without a taint of sham or exaggeration. She will love her child without spoiling it, I think. She does not make an uproar about her happiness either. The longer I live the more I suspect exaggerations. I fancy it is sometimes a sort of fashion for each to vie with the other in protestations about their wondrous felicity—and sometimes they *fib*! I am truly glad to hear you are all better at B——. In the course of three or four weeks now I expect to get leave to come to you. I certainly long to see you again. One circumstance reconciles me to this delay—the weather. I do not know whether it has been as bad with you as with us; but here for three weeks we have had little else than a succession of hurricanes.... You inquire after Mrs. Gaskell. She has not been here, and I think I should not like her to come now till summer. She is very busy now with her story of "North and South." I must make this note very short. Arthur joins me in sincere good wishes for a happy Christmas and many of them to you and yours. He is well, thank God, and so am I; and he *is* "my dear boy" certainly—dearer now than he was six months ago. In three days we shall actually have been married that length of time.

There was not much time for literary labours during these happy months of married life. The wife, new to her duties, was engaged in mastering them with all the patience, self-suppression, and industry which had characterised her throughout her life. Her husband was now her first thought; and he took the time which had formerly been devoted to reading, study, thought, and writing. But occasionally the pressure she was forced to put upon herself was very severe. Mr. Nicholls had never been attracted towards her by her literary fame; with literary effort, indeed, he had no sympathy, and upon the whole he would rather that his wife should lay aside her pen entirely than that she should gain any fresh triumphs in the world of letters. So she submitted, and with cheerful courage repressed that "gift" which had been her solace in sorrows deep and many. Yet once "the spell" was too strong to be resisted, and she hastily wrote a few pages of a new story called "Emma," in which once more she proposed to deal with her favourite theme—the history of a friendless girl. One would fain have seen how she would have treated her subject, now that "the colour of her thoughts" had been changed, and that a happy marriage had introduced her to a new phase of that life which she had studied so closely and so constantly. But it was not to be. On January 19, when she had returned to Haworth, after a visit to Sir J. K. Shuttleworth's, she wrote to her friend as follows. This letter was the last written in ink to her schoolfellow:

Haworth, January 19th, 1855.

Since our return from Gawthorpe we have had Mr. B——, one of Arthur's cousins, staying with us. It was a great pleasure. I wish you could have seen him and made his acquaintance: a true gentleman by nature and cultivation is not, after all, an everyday thing.... I very much wish to come to B——, and I hoped to be able to write with certainty and fix Wednesday, the 31st January, as the day; but the fact is I am not sure whether I shall be well enough to leave home. At present I should be a most tedious visitor. My health has really been very good ever since my return from Ireland, till about ten days ago. Indigestion and continual faint sickness have been my portion ever since. I never before felt as I have done lately. I am rather mortified to lose my good looks and grow thin as I am doing, just when I thought of going to B——. Poor J——! I still hope he will get better, but A—— writes grievous though not always clear or consistent accounts.

Dear Ellen, I want to see you, and I hope I shall see you well.

Those around her were not alarmed at first. They hoped that before long all would be well with her again; they could not believe that the joys of which she had just begun to taste were about to be snatched away. But her weakness grew apace; the sickness knew no abatement; and a deadly fear began to creep into the hearts of husband and father. She was soon so weak that she was compelled to remain in bed, and from that "dreary bed" she wrote two or three faint pencil notes which still exist—the last pathetic chapters in that life-long correspondence from which we have gathered so many extracts. In one of them, which Mrs. Gaskell has published, she says: "I want to give you an assurance which I know will comfort you—and that is that I find in my husband the tenderest nurse, the kindest support, the best earthly comfort that ever woman had. His patience never fails, and it is tried by sad days and broken nights." In another, the last, she says: "I cannot talk—even to my dear, patient, constant Arthur I can say but few words at once." One dreary March morning, when frost still bound the earth and no spring sun had come to gladden the hearts of those who watched for summer, her friend received another letter, written, not in the neat, minute hand of Charlotte Brontë, but in her father's tremulous characters:

Haworth, near Keighley,
March 30th, 1855.

My dear Madam,—We are all in great trouble, and Mr. Nicholls so much so that he is not sufficiently strong and composed as to be able to write. I therefore devote a few lines to tell you that my dear daughter is very ill, and apparently on the verge of the grave. If she could speak she would no doubt dictate to us whilst answering your kind letter. But we are left to ourselves to give what answer we can. The doctors have no hope of her case, and fondly as we a long time cherished hope, that hope is now gone; and we have only to look forward to the solemn event with prayer to God that He will give us grace and strength sufficient unto our day.

Ever truly and respectfully yours,

P. Brontë.

The following day, March 31st, 1855, the blinds were drawn once again at Haworth Parsonage; the last and greatest of the children of the house had passed away; and the brilliant name of Charlotte Brontë had become a name and nothing more! "We are left to ourselves," said Mr. Brontë in the letter I have just quoted—and so it was. Not the glory only, but the light, had fled from the parsonage where the childless father and the widowed husband sat together beside their dead. Of all the drear and desolate spots upon that wild Yorkshire moorland there was none now so dreary and so desolate as the house which had once been the home of Charlotte Brontë.

XII.

POSTHUMOUS HONOURS.

There is a deeper truth in the maxim which bids us judge no man happy till his death than most of us are apt to perceive. For sometimes the happiness of a life is crowned by death itself; and that which to the superficial gaze seems but the dreary and tragic close of the play, is really the welcome release from the burden which had become too heavy to be borne longer. But where life and breath fail suddenly in the moment of fullest hope, apparently in the moment also of greatest bliss, the strain upon our faith is almost too severe, and blinded and bewildered, we see nothing and feel nothing but the awful stroke of fate which has laid the loved one low, and the great gap which remains at the table and the hearth. It was with such a feeling as this that the outer world heard of that Easter-day tragedy which had been enacted to the bitter end among the Yorkshire hills. Those who knew the little household at Haworth had been watching, as has already been told, for that fulness of joy which seemed close at hand. They had seen the lonely authoress developing into the trustful happy wife, and they looked forward to no distant day when children should be gathered at her knee, and a new generation, born amid happier circumstances, freed from the strain and stress which had been laid upon her, should perpetuate a great name, and perhaps something of a great genius.

The announcement that all these hopes had been brought to nothing fell upon the world as a blow not easily to be borne. When it was made known that the author of "Jane Eyre" was dead, there rose up even from those who had been her bitter critics during her lifetime, a cry of pain and regret which would have astonished nobody more than herself had she been able to hear it. The genuine unaffected modesty which had enabled her to preserve the simplicity of her character amid all the temptations which thronged round her at the height of her fame, had prevented her from ever feeling herself to be a person of consequence in the world. What she did in the way of writing she did because she could not escape the commanding authority of her own genius; but the idea that by doing this she had made herself conspicuously great never once occurred to her. There is not a letter extant from her which shows that she thought anything of the fame or the fortune she had acquired. On the contrary everything that remains of her inner life proves that to the very last she esteemed herself as humbly as ever she did during the days of her "governessing" in Yorkshire or at Brussels. She knew of course that she attracted attention wherever she went; but her own unfeigned belief seems to have been that this attention was due solely to curiosity, and to curiosity of a not very pleasant or flattering kind. Brought up as she had been among those who regarded any literary pursuit, and above all the writing of a book, as something beyond the proper limits of the rights and duties of her sex, she had never quite escaped from the notion that in putting pen to paper she was in some vague way offending against the proprieties of society. It has been shown by an extract from one of her letters, how keenly and indignantly she repudiated the notion that she had ever written anything of which she needed to be ashamed. Her pure heart vindicated her absolutely upon that point. But, from first to last, she seemed during her literary career to feel that in writing novels she had sinned against the conventional canons, and that she was in consequence looked upon not as a great woman who had taken a lofty place in the republic of letters, but as a social curiosity who had done something which made her for the time-being notorious. How ready she was to forget her success as a writer is shown by a thousand passages in her correspondence, many of these passages being too tender or sacred for quotation. It is impossible to read her letters without seeing that, with the exception of a solitary friend, the companions of her daily life in Yorkshire did not feel at all drawn towards her by her literary fame. With her accustomed humility she accepted herself at their valuation, and whilst the nations afar off were praising her, she herself was perfectly ready to take a humble place in the circle of her friends at home. The tastes of her husband had unquestionably something to do in maintaining this simple and sincere modesty up to the end of her life. He was resolute in putting aside all thought of her literary achievements; his whole anxiety—an anxiety arising almost entirely from his desire for her happiness—was that she should cease entirely to be the author, and should become the busy, useful, contented wife of the village clergyman. It would be wrong to hide the fact that she was compelled to place a severe strain upon herself in order to comply with her husband's wishes; and once, as we have seen, her strength of self-repression gave way, and she indulged in the forbidden luxury of work with the pen. But it is not surprising that, surrounded by those who, loving her very dearly, yet withheld from her all recognition of her position as one of the great writers of the day, she should have accepted their estimate of her place with characteristic humility, and believed herself to be of little or no account outside the walls of her own home.

In this belief she lived and died. Among the letters before me, but from which I must forbear to quote, are not a few written during that last sad illness when the end began to loom before her vision. In these, whilst there are many anxious inquiries after the friends of early days, and many remarks upon their varying fortunes, many allusions, too, to her husband and father, and to parish work at Haworth, there is not a line which speaks of her own feelings as an author, or of the work which she had accomplished during the brief closing years of her life. The novelist has passed entirely out of sight, and only the wife, the friend, the expectant mother, remains. I know nothing which more touchingly shows one how small a thing is great fame, how little even the most marked and marvellous successes can affect the realities of life, than the last chapters of Charlotte Brontë's correspondence do. Her death, all unknown to the great world outside; her quiet funeral, treated only as the funeral of the clergyman's daughter, the curate's wife; the modest announcement of her end sent to the local papers—all these are in keeping with her own low estimate of herself.

But death, the great touchstone of humanity, revealed her true position to the world, and to her surviving relatives and friends. Copies of the newspapers of that sad March week in 1855 lie before me, carefully treasured up by loving hands. They speak with an eloquence which is not always that of mere words, of a nation's mourning for a great soul gone prematurely to its account. Of all these tributes of loving admiration, there are two which must be singled out for special mention. One is Miss Martineau's generous though not wholly satisfactory notice of "Currer Bell" in *The Daily News*, and the other the far more sympathetic article by "Shirley," which appeared in *Fraser's Magazine* a few months later.

Her father, her husband, her life-long friend, were wonderfully touched and moved when they found how closely the simple, modest woman, who had been so long a sweet and familiar presence to them, had wound herself round the great heart of the reading public. But they were slow to grasp all the truth. When it was proposed that some record of this noble life should be preserved, and when Mrs. Gaskell was named as the fittest among all Charlotte's literary acquaintances to undertake the office, there was strong and keen opposition on the part of those who had been nearest and dearest to her. With a natural feeling, to which no word of blame can be attached, but which again throws light upon the character of her surroundings in life, they objected to any revelation to the world of the real character and career of the lost member of their household. Happily, their scruples were overcome, and the world was permitted to read the story of the Brontës as told by one who was herself a woman of genius and of the highest moral worth. The reader of this monograph will not, it is to be hoped, imagine that the writer has presumed to set himself up as a rival to Mrs. Gaskell. He can no more pretend to equal her in the treatment of his subject than in the freshness of the interest attaching to it. And if he has found himself obliged to differ from her on some points not wholly unimportant, it must be borne in mind that the writer of to-day is free from not a few of the difficulties and restraints which weighed upon the writer of twenty years ago. Mrs. Gaskell had, indeed, to labour under serious disadvantages in her task. Not only was she unable to obtain full and ready access to all the materials which she needed to employ, but she was also compelled to introduce much irrelevant and even hurtful matter into a delightful and beautiful story. When, after gathering up the bare outline of the life she proposed to write, she complained to Mr. Brontë that there were not incidents enough in the history of his daughter to make an interesting narrative of the ordinary length, his reply was a characteristic one: "If there are not facts enough in Charlotte's life to make a book, madam, you must invent some." There is no need to say that Mrs. Gaskell declined to follow this advice; but none the less was she hampered all through her work by the necessity of introducing topics which had but little to do with her main theme; and we see the result in the fact that the plain unadorned tale of Charlotte Brontë and her sisters has been interwoven with dismal episodes with which properly it had no concern.

The publication of Mrs. Gaskell's biography came, however, as a revelation upon the world. Readers everywhere had learned to admire the writings of "Currer Bell," and to mourn over the premature extinction of her genius, but few of them had imagined that the life and personal character of the author of "Jane Eyre" had been what it was.

The following letter from Charles Kingsley to Mrs. Gaskell

sufficiently indicates the revulsion of feeling wrought in many minds by the publication of the "Memoir:"

St. Leonards, May 14, 1857.

Let me renew our long-interrupted acquaintance by complimenting you on poor Miss Brontë's "Life." You have had a delicate and a great work to do, and you have done it admirably. Be sure that the book will do good. It will shame literary people into some stronger belief that a simple, virtuous, practical home life, is consistent with high imaginative genius; and it will shame, too, the prudery of a not over cleanly though carefully white-washed age, into believing that purity is now (as in all ages till now) quite compatible with the knowledge of evil. I confess that the book has made me ashamed of myself. "Jane Eyre" I hardly looked into, very seldom reading a work of fiction—yours, indeed, and Thackeray's, are the only ones I care to open. "Shirley" disgusted me at the opening, and I gave up the writer and her books with a notion that she was a person who liked coarseness. How I misjudged her! and how thankful I am that I never put a word of my misconceptions into print, or recorded my misjudgments of one who is a whole heaven above me.

Well have you done your work, and given us the picture of a valiant woman made perfect by sufferings. I shall now read carefully and lovingly every word she has written, especially those poems, which ought not to have fallen dead as they did, and which seem to be (from a review in the current *Fraser*) of remarkable, strength and purity. [1]

The effect of the portrait was heightened by the admirable skill with which the background was drawn; and the story of the life gained a popularity which hardly any other recent English biography has attained. Yet, from the first, people were found here and there who, whilst acknowledging the skill, the sympathy, and the entire sincerity displayed by Mrs. Gaskell, yet whispered that the Charlotte Brontë of the story was not in all particulars the Charlotte Brontë they had known.

INTERIOR OF HAWORTH CHURCH.

One great change resulted immediately from the publication of Mrs. Gaskell's work. Haworth and its parsonage became the shrine to which hundreds of literary pilgrims from all parts of the globe began to find their way. To see the house in which the three sisters had spent their lives and done their work, to stand at the altar at which Charlotte was married, and beneath which her ashes now rest, and to hear her aged father preach one of his pithy, sensible, but dogmatic sermons, was what all literary lion-hunters aspired to do. In Yorkshire, indeed, the stolid people of the West Riding were not greatly moved by this enthusiasm. Just as Charlotte herself had seemed an ordinary and rather obscure person to her Yorkshire friends, so Haworth was still regarded as being a very dull and dreary village by those who lived near it. But the empire of genius knows no geographical boundaries, and if at her own doors Charlotte Brontë's sway was unrecognised, from far-distant quarters of the world there came the free and full acknowledgment of her power. No other land, however, furnished so many eager and enthusiastic visitors to the Brontë shrine as the United States, and the number of Americans who found their way to Haworth during the ten years immediately following the death of the author of "Jane Eyre" would, if properly recorded, astonish the world. The bleak and lonely house by the side of the moors, with its dismal little garden stretching down to the churchyard, where the village dead of many a generation rest, and its dreary out-look upon the old tower rising from its bank of nettles, the squalid houses of the hamlet, and the bare moorlands beyond, received almost as many visitors from the other side of the Atlantic during those years as Abbotsford or Stratford-upon-Avon. Mr. Brontë and Mr. Nicholls, though they were anxious to avoid the pertinacious intrusion of these curious but enthusiastic guests, could not entirely escape from meeting them. It followed that many an American lady and gentleman wandered through the rooms where the three sisters had dwelt together in love and unity, and where Charlotte had laboured alone after the light of her life had fled from her, and many an American magazine and newspaper contained the record of the impressions which these visits left upon the minds of those who made them.

In only one case does it seem necessary to recall those impressions. The late Mr. Raymond, for many years editor of *The New York Times*, visited Haworth, and wrote an account of his visit, some passages of which may well be reproduced here. He tells us how on his railway journey to Keighley, at that time the nearest railway station to Haworth, he "astonished an intelligent, sociable, and very agreeable English lady, his sole companion in the railway carriage, by telling her the errand which had brought him to Yorkshire. She lived in the neighbourhood, had read the 'Jane Eyre' novels, and 'supposed the girls were clever;' but 'she would not go ten steps to see where they lived, nor could she understand how a stranger from America should feel any interest in their affairs.'" Arrived at Haworth, and having satisfied himself as to the appearance of the parsonage and the character of the surrounding neighbourhood, Mr. Raymond went to the Black Bull Inn to dine and sleep. "As I took my candle to go to my chamber, I stepped for a moment into the kitchen, where the landlord and landlady were having a comfortable chat over pipes and ale, with a companionable rustic of the place, who proved to be a nephew of the old servant Tabby, who lived so long, and at last died in the service of the Brontë family. I joined the circle, and sat there till long after midnight. Branwell was clearly the hero of the village worship. A little red-headed fellow, the landlord said, quick, bright, abounding in stories, in jokes, and in pleasant talk of every kind; he was a general favourite in town, and the special wonder of the Black Bull circles. Small as he was, it was impossible to frighten him. They had seen him volunteer during a mill-riot to go in and thrash a dozen fellows, any one of whom could have put him in his pocket and carried him off at a minute's notice. Indeed a characteristic of the whole family seems to have been an entire insensibility to danger and to fear. Emily and Charlotte, these people told me, were one day walking through the street, when their great dog, Keeper, engaged in a fight with another dog of equal size. Whilst everybody else stood aloof and shouted, these girls went in, caught Keeper by the neck, and by dint of tugging, and beating him over the head, succeeded in dragging him away." I extract this passage because of the confirmation which it gives, on the authority of one who made his inquiries very soon after the death of Charlotte Brontë, of the account of some of the family characteristics which appear in these pages; nor will the story of Mr. Raymond's interview with

Mr. Brontë, told as it is with American directness, be without its interest and its value.

    The next morning I prepared to call at the parsonage. I was told that Mr. Brontë and Mr. Nicholls declined to receive strangers, having a great aversion to visits of curiosity, and being exceedingly retiring and reserved in their habits. I sent in my card, however, and was shown into the little library at the right of the entrance, where I was asked to await Mr. Nicholls's appearance. The room was small, very plainly furnished, with small bookcases round the walls, the one between the windows containing copies of the Brontë novels. Mr. Nicholls soon came in and made me welcome. To my apologies for my intrusion he assured me that while they were under the necessity of declining many visits, both he and his father were always happy to see their friends, and that the words "New York" upon my card were quite sufficient to insure me a welcome. Mr. Brontë, he said, was not up when I called, but had desired him to detain me until he could dress and come down, as he did soon after. I had an exceedingly pleasant conversation of half an hour with them both.... Mr. Brontë's personal appearance is striking and peculiar. He is tall, thin, and rather muscular, has a quick energetic manner, a reflective and by no means unpleasant countenance, and a resolute promptness of movement which indicated marked decision and firmness of character. The extraordinary stories told by Mrs. Gaskell of his inflammable temper, of his burning silk dresses belonging to his wife which he did not approve of her wearing, of his sawing chairs and tables, and firing off pistols in the back-yard by way of relieving his superfluous anger, find no warrant certainly in his present appearance, and are generally considered exaggerations. I remarked to him that I had been agreeably disappointed in the face of the country and the general aspect of the town, that they were less sombre and repulsive than Mrs. Gaskell's descriptions led me to expect. Mr. Nicholls and Mr. Brontë smiled at each other, and the latter remarked: "Well, I think Mrs. Gaskell tried to make us all appear as bad as she could." Mr. Brontë wears a very wide white neckcloth, and usually sinks his chin so that his mouth is barely visible over it. This gives him rather a singular expression, which is rendered still more so by spectacles with large round glasses enclosed in broad metallic rims. Though over eighty years old and somewhat infirm, he preaches once every Sunday in his church…. As I rose to take my leave Mr. Nicholls asked me to step into the parlour and look at Charlotte's portrait. It is the one from which the engraving in the "Life" is made; but the latter does no justice to the picture, which Mr. Nicholls said was a perfect likeness of the original. I remarked that the engraving gives to the face, and especially to the eyes, a weird, sinister, and unpleasant expression which did not appear in the portrait. He said he had observed it, and that nothing could be more unjust, for Charlotte's eyes were as soft and affectionate in their expression as could possibly be conceived.

Slight as these scraps from the pen of an American "interviewer" may seem, they have their value as contemporary records of scenes and incidents the memory of which is fast fading away. Yet even to-day old men and women are to be found in Haworth who can regale the curious stranger with many a reminiscence, more or less original, of the family which has given so great a glory to the place.

Mr. Brontë lived six years after the death of Charlotte. In spite of his great age he preached regularly in the church till within a few months of his death; and when at last he took to his bed, he retained his active interest in the affairs of the world. The newspapers which Charlotte mentions in one of her juvenile lucubrations as being regularly "taken in" at the patronage—*The Leeds Mercury* and *The Intelligencer*—were still brought to him, and read aloud. Every scrap of political information which he could gather up he cherished as a precious morsel; and any visitor who could tell him how the currents of public life were moving in the great West Riding towns around him, was certain to be welcome. But the chief enjoyment of his later years was connected with the public respect shown for his daughter's memory. The tributes to her virtues and her genius which were poured from the press after the publication of Mrs. Gaskell's work were valued by him to the latest moment of his life; and in the end he at last understood something of the character and the inner life of the child who had dwelt so long a stranger under her father's roof.

One point I must notice ere I quit the subject of Charlotte Brontë's father. Some of those who knew him in his later years, including one who is above all others entitled to an opinion on the subject, have objected to the portrait of him presented in these pages, as being over-coloured. So far as his early life and manhood are concerned, I cannot admit the force of the objection; for what has been told of Mr. Brontë in these pages has been gathered from the best of all sources—from the letters of his children and the recollections of those who saw much of him during that period. But it is perfectly true that in old age, after the marriage, and still more after the death of Charlotte, he was wonderfully softened in character. The fierce outburst of opposition to the engagement between his daughter and Mr. Nicholls was almost the last trace of that vehement passion which consumed him during his earlier years; and those visitors who, like Mr. Raymond, first became acquainted with him in the closing days of his life, found it difficult to believe that the stories told of his propensities in youth and middle-age could possibly be true. Time did its work at last, even on his adamantine character, softening the asperities, and wearing away the corners of a disposition, the angular eccentricities of which had long been so noticeable. Nor ought mention of the closing scenes of Mr. Brontë's life to be made without some reference to the part which Mr. Nicholls played at Haworth during those last sad years. The faithful husband remained under the parsonage roof in the character of a faithful son. The two men, bound together by so tender and sacred a tie, were not lightly to be separated, now that the living and visible link had been taken away. To some it may seem strange that Charlotte Brontë should have given her heart to one who was little disposed to sympathise with the overmastering passion inspired by her genius. But if in her husband she had found one who was not likely to have helped her in her literary work, she had also found in him a friend whose steadfastness even to the death was nobly proved. During all these sad and lonely years, whilst the father of the Brontës waited for the summons which should call him once more into their company, Charlotte's husband lived with him, the patient companion of his hours of pain and weariness, the faithful guardian of that living legacy which had been bequeathed to him by the woman whom he loved. And by this self-sacrificing life he did greater honour to the memory of Charlotte Brontë than by the most tender and vivid appreciation of her intellectual greatness.

There is a strange sad harmony between the closing chapter of the Brontë story and the earlier ones. The brightness had fled for ever from the parson's house; the gaiety which it had once witnessed was gone; even its fame as the home of one who was a living force in English literature had departed; but there still remained one to bear witness in his own person to the nobleness of that entire devotion to duty of the necessity of which Charlotte was so fully convinced. The friendship by which Mr. Nicholls soothed the last days of Mr. Brontë is a touching episode in the Haworth story, and it is one which cannot be allowed to pass unnoticed.

When Mr. Brontë died there was a general wish, not only among those who were impressed by the claims of all connected with his family upon Haworth, but by the parishioners themselves, that his son-in-law should succeed him, and that the relationship of the Brontës to the place where their lives had been spent and their work accomplished, should thus not be absolutely severed. But the bestowal of church patronage is not always influenced by considerations of this kind. The incumbency of Haworth was given to a stranger; Mr. Nicholls returned to Ireland; and new faces and a new life filled the parsonage-house in which "Jane Eyre" and "Wuthering Heights" were written.

THE ORGAN LOFT, OVER THE BRONTË TABLET AND PEW.

XIII.

THE BRONTË NOVELS.

The Brontë novels continued to sell largely for some time after Charlotte's death. The publication of Mrs. Gaskell's "Life" added not a little to the sale, and both at home and abroad the fame of the three sisters was greatly increased. But in recent years the disposition has been almost to ignore these books; and though fresh editions have recently been issued they have had no circulation worthy of being compared with that which they maintained between 1850 and 1860. Yet though there has not been the same interest in these remarkable performances as that which formerly prevailed, they continue from time to time to attract the attention of literary critics both in this and other countries, the works of "Currer Bell" naturally holding the foremost place in the critiques upon the writings of the sisters.

"Wuthering Heights," the solitary prose work of Emily Brontë, is now practically unread. Even those who admire the genius of the family, those who have the highest opinion of the qualities displayed in "Jane Eyre" or "Villette," turn away with something like a shudder from "that dreadful book," as one who knew the Brontës intimately always calls it. But I venture to invite the attention of my readers to this story, as being in its way as marvellous a *tour de force* as "Jane Eyre" itself. It is true that as a novel it is repulsive and almost ghastly. As one reads chapter after chapter of the horrible chronicles of Heathcliff's crimes, the only literary work that can be recalled for comparison with it is the gory tragedy of "Titus Andronicus." From the first page to the last there is hardly a redeeming passage in the book. The atmosphere is lurid and storm-laden throughout, only lighted up occasionally by the blaze of passion and madness. The hero himself is the most unmitigated villain in fiction; and there is hardly a personage in the story who is not in some shape or another the victim of mental or moral deformities. Nobody can pretend that such a story as this ever ought to have been written; nobody can read it without feeling that its author must herself have had a morbid if not a diseased mind. Much, however, may be said in defence of Emily Brontë's conduct in writing "Wuthering Heights." She was in her twenty-eighth year when it was written, and the reader has seen something of the circumstances of her life, and the motives which led her to take up her pen. The life had been, so far as the outer world could judge, singularly barren and unproductive. Its one eventful episode was the short visit to Brussels. But Brussels had made no such impression upon Emily as it made upon Charlotte. She went back to Haworth quite unchanged; her love for the moors stronger than ever; her self-reserve only strengthened by the assaults to which it had been exposed during her residence among strangers; her whole nature still crying out for the solitary life of home, and the sustenance which she drew from the congenial society of the animals she loved and the servants she understood. When, partly in the forlorn hope of making money by the use of her pen, but still more to give some relief to her pent-up feelings, she began to write "Wuthering Heights," she knew nothing of the world. "I am bound to avow," says Charlotte, "that she had scarcely more practical knowledge of the peasants amongst whom she lived than a nun has of the country people who sometimes pass her convent gates." Love, except the love for nature and for her own nearest relatives, was a passion absolutely unknown to her—as any one who cares to study the pictures of it in "Wuthering Heights" may easily perceive. Of harsh and brutal, or deliberate crime, she had no personal knowledge. She had before her, it is true, a sad instance of the results of vicious self-indulgence, and from that she drew materials for some portions of her story. But so far as the great movements of human nature were concerned—of those movements which are not to be mastered by book learning, but which must come as the tardy fruits of personal experience—she was in absolute ignorance. Little as Charlotte herself knew at this time of the world, and of men and women, she was an accomplished mistress of the secrets of life, in comparison with Emily.

When a woman has lived such a life as that of "Ellis Bell," her first literary effort must be regarded as the attempt of an innocent and ignorant child. It may be full of faults; all the conditions which should govern a work of art may have been neglected; the book itself, so far as story, tone, and execution are concerned, may be an entire mistake; but it will nevertheless give us far more insight into the real character of the author than any more elaborate and successful work, constructed after experience has taught her what to do and what to avoid in order to secure the ear of the public.

"Wuthering Heights," then, is the work of one who, in everything but years, was a mere child, and its great and glaring faults are to be forgiven as one forgives the mistakes of childhood. But how vast was the intellectual greatness displayed in this juvenile work! The author seizes the reader at the first moment at which they meet, holds him thrilled, entranced, terrified perhaps, in a grasp which never relaxes, and leaves him at last, after a perusal of the story, shaken and exhausted as by some great effort of the mind. Surely nowhere in modern English fiction can more striking proof be found of the possession of "the creative gift" in an extraordinary degree than is to be obtained in "Wuthering Heights." From what unfathomed recesses of her intellect did this shy, nervous, untrained girl produce such characters as those which hold the foremost place in her story? Mrs. Dean, the faithful domestic, we can understand; for her model was at Emily's elbow in the kitchen at Haworth. Joseph, the quaint High Calvinist, whose fidelity to his creed is unredeemed by a single touch of fellow-feeling with the human creatures around him, was drawn from life; and vigorous and powerful though his portrait is, one can understand it also. But Heathcliff, and the two Catherines, and Hareton Earnshaw—none of these ever came within the ken of Emily Brontë. No persons approaching them in originality or force of character were to be found in her circle of friends. Here and there some psychologist, learned in the secrets of morbid human nature, may have conceived the existence of such persons—evolved them from an inner consciousness which had been enlightened by years of studious labour. But no such slow and painful process guided the pen of Emily Brontë in painting these weird and wonderful portraits. They come forth with all the vigour and freshness, the living reality and impressiveness, which can belong only to the spontaneous creations of genius. They are no copies, indeed, but living originals, owing their lives to her own travail and suffering.

Regarded in this light they must, I think, be counted among the greatest curiosities of literature. Their very repulsiveness adds to their force. I have said that Heathcliff is the greatest villain in fiction. The reader of the story is disposed to echo the agonised cry of his wife when she asks: "Is Mr. Heathcliff a man? If so, is he mad? And if not, is he a devil?" It is not pleasant to see such a character obtruded upon us in a novel; but I repeat, it is far more difficult to paint a consummate villain of the Heathcliff type than to draw any of the more ordinary types of humanity. The concentration of power required in performing the task is enormous. At every moment the writer is tempted to turn aside and relieve the darkness by some touch of light; and the risk which the artist must encounter if he gives way to this temptation is that of destroying the whole effect of the picture. Light and shade there must be, or the portrait becomes a mere daub of blackness; and the man whom the author has desired to create stands forth as a monster, unrecognisable as a creature belonging to the same race as ourselves. But unless these lighter shades are introduced with a tact and a self-command which belong rather to genius than to art, there must, as I have said, be complete failure. Now, Emily Brontë has not failed in her portrait of Heathcliff. He stands, indeed, absolutely alone in that great human portrait-gallery which forms one of the chambers in the noble edifice of English literature. We can compare him to nobody else among the creatures of fiction. We cannot even trace his literary pedigree. He is a distinct being, not less original than he is hateful. But this circumstance does not alter the fact that we accept him at once as a real being, not a merely grotesque monster. He stands as much alone as Frankenstein's creature did; but we recognise within him that subtle combination of elements which gives him kinship with the human race. Here, then, Emily Brontë has succeeded; and girl as she was when she wrote, she has succeeded where some of the most practised writers have failed entirely. Compare "Wuthering Heights," for example, with the fantastic horrors of Lord Lytton's "Strange Story," and you feel at once how much more powerful and masterly is the touch of the woman. Lord Lytton's villain, though he has been drawn with so much care and skill, is often absurd and at last entirely wearisome. Emily Brontë's is consistent, terrible, fascinating, from beginning to end. Then, again, the writer never tries to frighten her reader with a bogey. She never hints at the possibility of supernatural agencies being at work behind the scene. Even when she is showing us that Heathcliff is for ever haunted by the dead Catherine, she makes it clear by the words she puts into his own mouth that his belief on the subject is nothing more than the delusion of a disordered brain, worried by a guilty conscience. "I knew no living thing in flesh and blood was by," says Heathcliff, describing how he dug down into Catherine's grave on the night after she had been buried; "but as certainly as you perceive the approach to some substantial body in the dark, so certainly I felt that Cathy was there: not under me, but on the earth. A sudden sense of relief flowed from my heart through every limb. I relinquished my labour of agony, and turned consoled at once—unspeakably consoled. Her presence was with me; it remained while I refilled the grave and led me home. You may laugh if you will; but I was sure I should see her there. I was sure she was with me, and I could not help talking to her. Having reached the Heights I rushed eagerly to the door. It was fastened; and I remember that accursed Earnshaw and my wife opposed my entrance. I remember stopping to kick the breath out of him, and then hurrying upstairs to my room and hers. I looked round impatiently—I felt her by me—I could *almost* see her, and yet I *could not*! I ought to have sweat blood then, from the anguish of my yearning—from the fervour of my supplications to have but one glimpse! I had not one. She showed herself, as she often was in life, a devil to me. And, since then, sometimes more and sometimes less, I've been the sport of that intolerable torture.... When I sat in the house with Hareton, it seemed that on going out I should meet her; when I walked on the moors I should meet her coming in. When I went from home I hastened to return. She *must* be somewhere at the Heights, I was certain! And when I slept in her chamber—I was beaten out of that. I couldn't lie there; for the moment I closed my eyes, she was either outside the window, or sliding back the panels, or entering the room, or even resting her darling head on the same pillow as she did when a child; and I must open my lids to see. And so I opened and closed them a hundred times a night—to be always disappointed!" Here is a picture of a man who is really haunted. No supernatural agency is invoked; no strain is put upon the reader's credulity. We are asked to believe in the suspension of no law of nature. In one word, we can all understand how a wicked man, whose brain has, as it were, been made drunk with the fumes of his own wickedness, can be persecuted throughout his whole life by terrors of this kind; and just because we are able to conceive and understand it, this haunting of Heathcliff by the ghost of his dead mistress is infinitely more terrible than if it had been accompanied either by the paraphernalia of rococo horrors which Mrs. Radcliffe habitually invoked, or by those refined and subtle supernatural phenomena which Lord Lytton employs in his famous ghost story.

This strict honesty which refused to allow the writer of the weirdest story in the English language to avail herself of the easiest of all the modes of stimulating a reader's terrors, is shown all through the novel. The workmanship is good from beginning to end, though the art is crude and clumsy. She never allows a date to escape her memory, nor are there any of those broken threads which usually abound in the works of inexperienced writers. All is neatly, clearly, carefully finished off. Every date fits into its place, and so does every incident. The reader is never allowed to wander into a blind alley. Though at the outset he finds himself in a bewildering maze, far too complicated in construction to comply with the canons of literary art, he has only to go straight on, and in the end he will find everything made plain. Emily permits no fact however minute to drop from her grasp. Irrelevant though it may seem at the moment when the reader meets with it, a place has been prepared for it in the edifice which the patient hands are rearing, and in the end it will be fitted into that place. Thus there is no scamped work in the story; nor any sacrifice of details in order to obtain those broad effects in which the tale abounds.

Let the reader turn to "Wuthering Heights," and he will find many a simple innocent revelation of the character of the author peeping out from its pages in unexpected places. We know how the story was written, and how day by day it was submitted to the revision of Charlotte and Anne. We may be sure under these circumstances that Emily did not allow too much of her true inner nature to appear in what she wrote. Even from her sisters she habitually concealed some of the strongest and deepest emotions of her heart. But such passages as the following, when read in the light of her history, as we know it now, are of strange and abiding interest:

> He said the pleasantest manner of spending a hot July

day was lying from morning till evening on a bank of heath in the middle of the moors, with the bees humming dreamily about among the bloom, and the larks singing high up over head, and the blue sky and bright sun shining steadily and cloudlessly. That was his most perfect idea of heaven's happiness. Mine was rocking in a rustling green tree, with a west wind blowing, and bright white clouds flitting rapidly above; and not only larks, but throstles and blackbirds and linnets and cuckoos, pouring out music on every side, and the moors seen at a distance broken into cool dusky dells; but close by great swells of long grass undulating in waves to the breeze; and woods and sounding water, and the whole world awake and wild with joy. He wanted all to lie in an ecstasy of peace. I wanted all to sparkle and dance in a glorious jubilee. I said his heaven would be only half alive; and he said mine would be drunk. I said I should fall asleep in his; and he said he could not breathe in mine.

For "he," read "Anne," and accept Emily as speaking for herself, and we have in this passage a vivid description of the opposing tastes of the two sisters.

The abhorrence which Charlotte felt for the High Calvinism, which was the favourite creed around her, was felt even more strongly by Emily. Her poems throw not a little light upon this feature of her character; but we also gain some from her solitary novel. Joseph, the old man-servant, was a study from life, and he represented one of a class whom the author thoroughly disliked, but for whom at the same time she entertained a certain respect. Again and again she breaks forth with all the force of sarcasm she can command against "the wearisomest, self-righteous pharisee that ever ransacked a Bible to rake the promises to himself and fling the curses to his neighbours." Yet there is no character in the story over whom she lingers more lovingly than Joseph, and it is only in painting his portrait that she allows herself to be betrayed into the display of any of that humour which, according to her sisters, always lurked very near the surface of her character, ever ready to show itself when no stranger was at hand. Few who have read "Wuthering Heights" can have forgotten Joseph's quaint remark when the boy Heathcliff has disappeared, and the others are speculating on his fate.

> Nay, nay, he's noan at Gimmerton. I's never wonder but he's at t' bottom of a bog-boile. This visitation worn't for nowt, and I wod hev ye to look out, miss. Yah muh be t' next. Thank Hivin for all! All works togither for gooid to them as is chozzen, and piked out fro' th' rubbidge. Yah knaw whet t' Scripture ses.

There is one passage in the story which furnishes so strange a foreshadowing of Emily's own death, that it is difficult to believe that she did not bear it in her mind during those last hours when she faced the dread enemy with such unwavering resolution. She is writing of the death of Mrs. Earnshaw.

> Poor soul! till within a week of her death that gay heart never failed her; and her husband persisted doggedly, nay furiously, in affirming her health improved every day. When Kenneth warned him that his medicines were useless at that stage of the malady, and he needn't put him to further expense by attending her, he retorted:

> "I know you need not. She's well; she does not want any more attendance from you! She never was in a consumption. It was a fever, and it is gone: her pulse is as slow as mine now, and her cheek as cool!"

> He told his wife the same story, and she seemed to believe him. But one night while leaning on his shoulder, in the act of saying she thought she should be able to get up to-

morrow, a fit of coughing took her—a very slight one—he raised her in his arms; she put her two hands about his neck, her face changed, and she was dead.

Strange and inscrutable, indeed, are the mysteries of the human heart! Let the reader turn from the passage I have quoted to that letter in which Charlotte laments that "Emily is too intractable," and let him read how she refused to believe that she was ill until death caught her as suddenly as it did the wife of Earnshaw. The blindness to the approach of danger, which she describes so clearly in her story, was but a few months afterwards displayed even more fully by herself. In this last quotation, which I venture to make from a book now seldom opened, we see the author speaking evidently out of the fulness of her heart on a subject on which in conversation she was specially reserved.

I don't know if it be a peculiarity in me, but I am seldom otherwise than happy when watching in the chamber of death, should no frenzied or despairing mourner share the duty with me. I see a repose that neither earth nor hell can break, and I feel an assurance of the endless and shadowless hereafter—the Eternity they have entered—where life is boundless in its duration, and love in its sympathy, and joy in its fulness. I noticed on that occasion how much selfishness there is even in a love like Mr. Linton's, when he so regretted Catherine's blessed release! To be sure, one might have doubted, after the wayward and impatient existence she had led, whether she merited a haven of peace at last. One might doubt in seasons of cold reflection; but not then in the presence of her corpse. It asserted its own tranquillity, which seemed a pledge of equal quiet to its former inhabitant.

Even these fragments, culled from the pages of "Wuthering Heights," are sufficient to show how little the story has in common with the ordinary novel. Differing widely in every respect from "Jane Eyre," dealing with characters and circumstances which belong to the romance rather than the reality of life, it is yet stamped by the same originality, the same daring, the same thoughtfulness, and the same intense individuality. It is a marvel to all who know anything of the secrets of literary work, that Haworth Parsonage should have produced "Jane Eyre;" but how is the marvel increased, when we know that at the same time it produced, from the brain of another inmate, the wonderful story of "Wuthering Heights." Brimful of faults as it may be, that book is alone sufficient to prove that a rare and splendid genius was lost to the world when Emily Brontë died.

All interested in the story of the Brontës must be curious to know whence Emily derived the materials for this romance. I have said that Heathcliff and the other prominent characters of the story are creations of her own; and indeed the book in its originality is almost unique. But this does not affect the fact that somewhere, and at some period during her life, the seed which brought forth this strange fruit must have been sown. It has been suggested by some—strangely ignorant, surely, of the conditions of West Riding life during the present century—that Emily obtained the skeleton of her plot from her own observation of people around her. But the life round Haworth was really tame and commonplace. Josephs and Mrs. Deans could be found in and about the village in abundance; but there were no people round whose lives hung anything of the mystery which attaches to Heathcliff. It was, so far as I can learn, during her early girlhood that Emily's mind was filled with those grim traditions which she afterwards employed in writing "Wuthering Heights." Mr. Brontë, in addition to his other gifts, had the faculty of storytelling highly developed, and his delight was to use this faculty in order to awaken superstitious terrors in the hearts of his children.

Though he habitually took his meals alone, he would often appear at the table where his daughters, with possibly their one female friend, were breakfasting, and, without joining in the repast, would entertain the little company of schoolgirls with wild legends not only relating to life in Yorkshire during the last century, but to that still wilder life which he had left behind him in Ireland. A cold smile would play round his mouth as he added horror to horror in his attempts to move his children; and his keen eyes sparkled with triumph when he found he had succeeded in filling them with alarm. Emily listened to these stories with bated breath, drinking them, in eagerly. She could repeat them afterwards by the hour together to her sisters; and no better proof of the deep root they took in her sensitive nature can be desired, than the fact that they led her to write "Wuthering Heights." Thus the paternal influence, strong as it was in the case of all the daughters, was peculiarly strong as regarded Emily; and we can gauge the nature of that influence in the weird and ghastly story which was brought forth under its shadow.

It is with a feeling of curious disappointment that one rises from the perusal of the writings of Anne Brontë. She wrote two novels, "Agnes Grey" and "The Tenant of Wildfell Hall," neither of which will really repay perusal. In the first she sought to set forth some of the experiences which had befallen her in that patient placid life which she led as a governess. They were not ordinary experiences, the reader should know. I have resolutely avoided, in writing this sketch of Charlotte Brontë and her sisters, all unnecessary reference to the tragedy of Branwell Brontë's life. But it is a strange sad feature of that story, that the pious and gentle youngest sister was compelled to be a closer and more constant witness of his sins and his sufferings than either Charlotte or Emily. She was living under the same roof with him when he went astray and was thrust out in deep disgrace. I have said already that the effect of his career upon her own was as strong and deep as Mrs. Gaskell represents it to have been. Branwell's fall formed the dark turning-point in Anne Brontë's life. So it was not unnatural that it should colour her literary labours. Accordingly, whilst "Agnes Grey" gives us some of the scenes of her governess life, dressed up in the fashion of the ordinary romances of thirty years ago, "The Tenant of Wildfell Hall" presents us with a dreary and repulsive picture of Branwell Brontë's condition after his fall. Charlotte, in her brief memoir of her sisters, does bare justice to Anne when she speaks in these words upon the subject:

> "The Tenant of Wildfell Hall," by "Acton Bell," had likewise an unfavourable reception. At this I cannot wonder. The choice of subject was an entire mistake. Nothing less congruous with the writer's nature could be conceived. The motives which dictated this choice were pure, but, I think, slightly morbid. She had in the course of her life been called on to contemplate, near at hand, and for a long time, the terrible effects of talents misused and faculties abused; hers was naturally a sensitive, reserved, and dejected nature; what she saw sank very deeply into her mind; it did her harm. She brooded over it till she believed it to be a duty to reproduce every detail (of course with fictitious characters, incidents, and situations) as a warning to others. She hated her work, but would pursue it. When reasoned with on the subject, she regarded such reasonings as a temptation to self-indulgence. She must be honest; she must not varnish, soften, or conceal. This well-meant resolution brought on her misconception and some abuse, which she bore, as it was her custom to bear whatever was unpleasant, with mild steady patience. She was a very sincere and practical Christian, but the tinge of religious melancholy communicated a sad hue to her brief blameless life.

What a picture one gets of this third and least considered of the Brontë sisters in the passage which I have quoted! A lovable, fair-featured girl, leading a blameless life, lighted up by few hopes of any brighter future—for the one little romance of her own heart had been destroyed ere this by the unrelenting hand of death—and not inspired as her sisters were by the passion of the artist or the creator; a girl whose simple faith was still unmoved from its first foundations; whose delight was in visiting the poor and helping the sick, who had no sustaining conviction of her own strength such as maintained Charlotte and Emily in their darkest hours, and whose very piety was "tinged with melancholy." This is the girl who, not from any of the irresistible impulses which attend the exercise of the creative faculty, but from a simple sense of duty, set herself the hard task of depicting in the pages of a novel the consequences of a shocking vice with which her brother's degradation had brought her into close and abiding contact. Of course she failed. It is not by hands so weak as those of Anne Brontë that effective blows are struck at such sins as she assailed. But whilst we acknowledge her failure, let us do justice both to the self-sacrificing courage and the fervent piety which led her to undertake this painful work.

Of Charlotte Brontë's novels, as a whole, I shall say nothing at this point; but something may very properly be said here of the story which she wrote at the time when her sisters were engaged in writing "Wuthering Heights" and "Agnes Grey." It was not published until after her death, and after the world had learned from Mrs. Gaskell's pages something of the truth about her life. Its interest to the ordinary reader was to a considerable extent discounted by the fact that the author had so largely used the materials in her last great work, "Villette." But even as a mere novel "The Professor" has striking merits, and would well repay perusal from that point of view alone; whilst as a means of gaining fresh light with regard to the character of the writer, it is not less valuable than "Wuthering Heights" itself. True, "The Professor" is not really a first attempt. "A first attempt it certainly was not," says Charlotte in reference to it, "as the pen which wrote it had previously been worn a good deal in a practice of some years." But the previous writings, of which hardly a trace now remains—those early MSS. having been carefully destroyed, with the exception of the few which Mrs. Gaskell was permitted to see—were in no respect finished productions, nor had they been written with a view to publication. The first occasion on which Charlotte Brontë really began a prose work which she proposed to commit to the press was on that day when, seated by her two sisters, she joined them in penning the first page of a new novel.

To all practical intents, therefore, "The Professor" is entitled to be regarded as a first work; and certainly nothing can show Charlotte's peculiar views on the subject of novel-writing more clearly or strikingly than this book does. The world knows how resolutely in all her writings she strove to be true to life as she saw it. In "Jane Eyre" there are, indeed, romantic incidents and situations, but even in that work there is no trespassing beyond the limits always allowed to the writer of fiction; whilst it must not be forgotten that "Jane Eyre" was in part a response to the direct appeal from the publishers for something different in character from "The Professor." In that first story she determined that she would write a man's life as men's lives usually are. Her hero was "never to get a shilling he had not earned;" no sudden turns of fortune were "to lift him in a moment to wealth and high station;" and he was not even to marry "a beautiful girl or a lady of rank." "As Adam's son he should share Adam's doom, and drain throughout life a mixed and moderate cup of enjoyment."

Very few novel-readers will share this conception of what a novel ought to be. The writer of fiction is an artist whose accepted duty it is to lift men and women out of the cares of ordinary life, out of the sordid surroundings which belong to every lot in this world, and to show us life under different, perhaps under fantastic, conditions: a life which by its contrast to that we ourselves are leading shall furnish some relief to our mental vision, wearied and jaded by its constant contemplation of the fevers and disappointments, the crosses and long years of weary monotony, which belong to life as it is. We know how a great living writer has ventured to protest against this theory, and how in her finest works of fiction she has shown us life as it is, under the sad and bitter conditions of pain, sorrow, and hopelessness. But Charlotte Brontë wrote "The Professor" long before "George Eliot" took up her pen; and she must at least receive credit for having been in the field as a reformer of fiction before her fellow-labourer was heard of.

She was true to the conditions she had laid down for herself in writing "The Professor." Nothing more sober and matter-of-fact than that story is to be found in English literature. And yet, though the landscape one is invited to view is but a vast plain, without even a hillock to give variety to the prospect, it has beauties of its own which commend it to our admiration. The story, as everybody knows, deals with Brussels, from which she had just returned when she began to write it. But it is sad to note the difference between the spirit of "The Professor" and that which is exhibited in "Villette." Dealing with the same circumstances, and substantially with the same story, the author has nevertheless cast each in a mould of its own. Nor is the cause of this any secret to those who know Charlotte Brontë. When she wrote "The Professor," disillusioned though she was, she was still young, and still blessed with that fervent belief in a better future which the youthful heart can never quite cast out, even under the heaviest blows of fate. She had come home restless and miserable, feeling Haworth to be far too small and quiet a place for her; and her mind could not take in the reality that under that modest roof the remainder of her life was destined to be spent. Suffering and unhappy as she was, she could not shut out the hope that brighter days lay before her. The fever of life racked her; but in the very fact that it burnt so high there was proof that love and hope, the capacity for a large enjoyment of existence, still lived within her. So "The Professor," though a sad, monotonous book, has life and hope, and a fair faith in the ultimate blessedness of all sorrowful ones, shining through all its pages; and it closes in a scene of rest and peace.

Very different is the case with "Villette." It was written years after the period when "The Professor" was composed, when the hard realities of life had ceased to be veiled under tender mists of sentiment or imagination, and when the lonely present, the future, "which often appals me," made the writer too painfully aware that she had drunk the cup of existence almost to the dregs. As a piece of workmanship there is no comparison between it and the earlier story. On every page we see traces of the artist's hand. Genius flashes forth from both works it is true, but in "Villette" it is genius chastened and restrained by a cultivated taste, or working under that high pressure which only the trained writer can bring to bear upon it. Yet, whilst we must admit the immense superiority of the later over the earlier work, we cannot turn from the one to the other without being painfully touched by the sad, strange difference in the spirit which animates them. The stories, as I have said, are nearly the same. With some curious transformations, in fact, they are practically identical. But they are only the same in the sense in which the portrait of the fair and hopeful girl, with life's romance shining before her eyes, is the same as the portrait of the worn and solitary woman for whom the romance is at an end. A whole world of suffering, of sorrow, of patient endurance, lies between the two. I have spoken of the mood in which "The Professor" was written—Hope still lingered at that time in the heart, breathing its merciful though illusory suggestions of something brighter and better in the future. All who have passed through the ordeal of a life's sorrow will be able to understand the distinction between the temperament of the author at that period in her life, and her temperament when she composed "Villette." For such suffering ones know, how, in the first and bitterest moment of sorrow, the heart cannot shut out the blessed belief that a time of release from the pain will come—a time far off, perhaps, but in which a day bright as that which has suddenly been eclipsed will shine again. It is only as the years go by, and as the first ache of intolerable anguish has been lulled into a dreary rest by habit, that the faith which gave them strength to bear the keenest smart, takes flight, and leaves them to the pale monotony of a twilight which can know no dawn. It was in this later and saddest stage of endurance that "Villette" was written. The sharpest pangs of the heart-experiences at Brussels had vanished. The author, no longer full of the self-consciousness of the girl, could even treat her own story, her own sorrows of that period, with a lighter hand, a more artistic touch, than when she first wrote of them; but through all her work there ran the dreary conviction that in those days of mingled joy and suffering she had tasted life at its best, and that in the future which lay before her there could be nothing which should renew either the strong delights or keen anguish of that time. So the book is pitched, as we know, in a key of almost absolute hopelessness. Nothing but the genius of Charlotte Brontë could have saved such a work from sinking under its own burden of gloom. That this intense and tragic study of a soul should have had power to fascinate, not the psychologist alone, but the vast masses of the reading world, is a triumph which can hardly be paralleled in recent literary efforts. In "The Professor" we move among the same scenes, almost among the same characters and incidents, but the whole atmosphere is a different one. It is a dull, cold atmosphere, if you will, but one feels that behind the clouds the sun is shining, and that sooner or later the hero and heroine will be allowed to bask in his reviving rays. Set the two stories together, and read them in the light of all that passed between the years in which they were written—the death of Branwell, of Emily, and of Anne, the utter shattering of some fair illusions which buoyed up Charlotte's heart in the first years of her literary triumph, the apparent extinction of all hope as to future happiness—and you will get from them a truer knowledge of the author's soul than any critic or biographer could convey to you.

Ere I part from "The Professor," which, naturally enough, never gained much attention from the public, I must extract from it one passage, a parallel to which may be found in many of Charlotte Brontë's letters. It describes, as none but one who had suffered could do, one of those seasons of mental depression, arising from bodily illness, by which she was visited at intervals, and under the influence of which not a little of her work was done. Reading it, we get some idea of the true origin of much in her character that was supposed to be morbid and unnatural:

> Man is ever clogged with his mortality, and it was my mortal nature which now faltered and plained; my nerves which jarred and gave a false sound, because the soul, of late rushing headlong to an aim, had overstrained the body's comparative weakness. A horror of great darkness fell upon me; I felt my chamber invaded by one I had known formerly but had thought for ever departed. I was temporarily a prey to hypochondria. She had been my acquaintance, nay, my guest, once before in boyhood; I had entertained her at bed and board for a year; for that space of time I had her to myself in secret; she lay with me, she ate with me, she walked out with me, showing me nooks in woods, hollows in hills, where we could sit together, and where she could drop her drear veil over me, and so hide sky and sun, grass and green tree; taking me entirely to her death-cold bosom and holding me with arms of bone. What tales she would tell me at such hours! What songs she would recite in my ears! How she would discourse to me of her own country—the grave—and again and again promise to conduct me there ere long; and drawing me to the very brink of a black sullen river, show me on the other side shores unequal with mound, monument, and tablet, standing up in a glimmer more hoary than moonlight. "Necropolis!" she would whisper, pointing to the pale piles, and add, "it contains a mansion prepared for you." But my boyhood was lonely, parentless; uncheered by brother or sister; and there was no marvel that, just as I rose to youth, a sorceress, finding me lost in vague mental wanderings, with many affections and few objects, glowing aspirations and gloomy prospects,

strong desires and tender hopes, should lift up her illusive lamp to me in the distance, and lure me to her vaulted home of horrors.

It was when, under the influence of occasional spells of physical suffering such as she here describes, that Miss Brontë gave those who saw her the impresion that her mind was naturally a morbid one; and, as I have said before, the same influence is at times perceptible in her writings. One of the purposes with which this little book has been written is to show the world how much of the gloom and depression which are now associated with her story, must be attributed to purely physical or accidental causes.

XIV.

CONCLUSION.

No apology need be offered for any single feature of Charlotte Brontë's life or character. She was what God made her in the furnace of sore afflictions and yet more sore temptations; her life, instinct with its extraordinary individuality, was, notwithstanding, always subject to exterior influences for the existence of which she was not responsible, and which more than once threatened to change the whole nature and purpose of her being; her genius, which brought forth its first-fruits under the cold shade of obscurity and adversity, was developed far more largely by sorrow, loneliness, and pain, than by the success which she gained in so abundant a degree. There are features of her character which we can scarcely comprehend, for the existence of which we are unable to account; and there are features of her genius which jar upon our sympathies and ruffle our conventional ideas; but for neither will one word of apology or excuse be offered by any who really know and love this great woman.

The fashion which exalted her to such a pinnacle of fame, like many another fashion, has lost its vogue; and the present generation, wrapped in admiration of another school of fiction, has consigned the works of "Currer Bell" to a premature sepulchre. But her friends need not despair; for from that dreary tomb of neglect an hour of resurrection must come, and the woman who has given us three of the most masterful books of the century, will again assert her true position in the literature of her country. We hear nothing now of the "immorality" of her writings. Younger people, if they turn from the sparkling or didactic pages of the most popular of recent stories to "Jane Eyre" or "Villette," in the hope of finding there some stimulant which may have power to tickle their jaded palates, will search in vain for anything that even borders upon impropriety—as we understand the word in these enlightened days—and they will form a strange conception of the generation of critics which denounced "Currer Bell" as the writer of immoral works of fiction. But it is said that there is coarseness in her stories, "otherwise so entirely noble." Even Mrs. Gaskell has assented to the charge; and it is generally believed that Charlotte Brontë, as a writer, though not immoral in tone, was rude in language and coarse in thought. The truth, I maintain, is, that this so-called coarseness is nothing more than the simplicity and purity, the straightforwardness and unconsciousness which an unspotted heart naturally displays in dealing with those great problems of life which, alas! none who have drunk deep of the waters of good and evil can ever handle with entire freedom from embarrassment. An American writer [2] has spoken of Charlotte Brontë as "the great pre-Raphaelite among women, who was not ashamed or afraid to utter what God had shown her, and was too single-hearted of aim to swerve one hairbreadth in duplicating nature's outlines." She was more than this however; she was bold enough to set up a standard of right of her own; and when still the unknown daughter of the humble Yorkshire parson, she could stir the hearts of readers throughout the world with the trumpet-note of such a declaration as this: "Conventionality is not morality; self-righteousness is not religion; to pluck the mask from the face of the Pharisee is not to lift an impious hand to the Crown of Thorns." Let it be remembered that these words were written nearly thirty years ago, when conventionalism was still a potent influence in checking the free utterance of our inmost opinions; and let us be thankful that in that heroic band to whom we owe the emancipation of English thought, a woman holds an honourable place.

Writing of her life just after it had closed, her friend Miss Martineau said of her: "In her vocation she had, in addition to the deep intuitions of a gifted woman, the strength of a man, the patience of a hero, and the conscientiousness of a saint." Those who know her best will apply to her personal character the epithets which Miss Martineau reserved for her career as an author. It has been my object in these pages to supplement the picture painted in Mrs. Gaskell's admirable biography by the addition of one or two features, slight in themselves perhaps, and yet not unimportant when the effect of the whole as a faithful portrait is considered. Charlotte Brontë was not naturally a morbid person; in youth she was happy and high-spirited; and up to the last moment of her life she had a serene strength and cheerfulness which seldom deserted her, except when acute physical suffering was added to her mental pangs. If her mind could have been freed from the depressing influences exerted on it by her frail and suffering body, it would have been one of the healthiest and most equable minds of our age. As it was, it showed itself able to meet the rude buffetings of fate without shrinking and without bravado; and the woman who is to this day regarded by the world at large as a marvel of self-conscious genius and of unchecked morbidness, was able to her dying hour to take the keenest, liveliest interest in the welfare of her friends, to pour out all her sympathy wherever she believed it was needed and deserved, and to lighten the grim parsonage of Haworth by a presence which, in the sacred recesses of her home, was bright and cheerful, as well as steadfast and calm.

"Do not underrate her oddity," said a gifted friend who knew her during her heyday of fame, while these pages were being written. Her oddity, it must be owned, was extreme—so far as the world could judge. But I have striven to show how much this eccentricity was outward and superficial only, due in part to the peculiar conditions of her early life, but chiefly to the excessive shyness in the presence of strangers which she shared with her sisters. At heart, as some of these letters will show, she was one of the truest women who ever breathed; and her own heart-history was by no means so exceptional, so far removed from the heart-history of most women, as the public believes.

The key to her character was simple and unflinching devotion to duty. Once she failed, or rather, once she allowed inclination to blind her as to the true direction of the path of duty, and that single failure coloured the whole of her subsequent life. But her own condemnation of herself was more sharp and bitter than any which could have been passed upon her by the world, and from that one venial error she drew lessons which enabled her henceforward to live with a steady, constant power of self-sacrifice at her command such as distinguishes saints and heroes rather than ordinary men and women. Hot, impulsive, and tenacious in her affections, she suffered those whom she loved the most dearly to be torn from her without losing faith in herself or in God; tenderly sensitive as to the treatment which her friends received, she repaid the cruelty and injustice of her father towards the man whose heart she had won, by a depth of devotion and self-sacrifice which can only be fully estimated by those who know under what bitter conditions it was lavished upon an unworthy parent; bound, as all the children of genius are, by the spell of her own imagination, she was yet able during the closing months of her life to lay aside her pen, and give herself up wholly, at the desire of her husband, to those parish duties which had such slight attractions for her. Those who, knowing these facts, still venture to assert that the virtues which distinguished "Currer Bell" the author were lacking in Charlotte Brontë the woman, must have minds warped by deep-rooted and unworthy prejudices.

I have expressed my conviction that the comparative neglect from which "Jane Eyre" and its sister-works now suffer is only temporary. It is true that in some respects these books are not attractive. Though they are written with a terse vigour which must make them grateful to all whose palates are cloyed by the pretty writing of the present generation, they undoubtedly err on the side of a lack of literary polish. And though the portraits presented to us in their pages are wonderful as works of art, unsurpassed as studies of character, the range of the artist is a limited one, and, as a rule, the subjects chosen are not the most pleasing that could have been conceived. Yet one great and striking merit belongs to this masterly painter of men and women, which is lacking in some who, treading to a certain extent in her footsteps, have achieved even a wider and more brilliant reputation. There is no taint of the dissecting-room about her books; we are never invited to admire the supreme cleverness of the operator who, with unsparing knife, lays bare before us the whole cunning mechanism of the soul which is stretched under the scalpel; nor are we bidden to pause and listen to those didactic moralisings which belong rather to the preacher or the lecturer than the novelist. It is the artist, not the anatomist who is instructing us; and after all, we may derive a more accurate knowledge of men and women as they are from the cartoons of a Raphael than from the most elaborate diagrams or sections of the most eminent of physiologists.

Perhaps no merit is more conspicuous in Charlotte Brontë's writings than their unswerving honesty. Writing always "under the spell," at the dictation, as it were, of an invisible and superior spirit, she would never write save when "the fit was upon her" and she had something to say. "I have been silent lately because I have accumulated nothing since I wrote last," is a phrase which fell from her on one occasion. Save when she believed that she had accumulated something, some truth which she was bound to convey to the world, she would not touch her pen. She had every temptation to write fast and freely. Money was needed at home, and money was to be had by the mere production of novels which, whether good, bad, or indifferent, were certain to sell. But she withstood the temptation bravely, withstood it even when it came strengthened by the supplications of her friends; and from first to last she gave the world nothing but her best. This honesty—rare enough unfortunately among those whose painful lot it is to coin their brains into money—was carried far beyond these limits. When in writing she found that any character had escaped from her hands—and every writer of fiction knows how easily this may happen—she made no attempt to finish the portrait according to the canons of literary art. She waited patiently for fresh light; studying deeply in her waking hours, dreaming constantly of her task during her uneasy slumbers, until perchance the light she needed came and she could go on. But if it came not she never pretended to supply the place of this inspiration of genius by any clever trick of literary workmanship. The picture was left unfinished—perfect so far as it went, but broken off at the point at which the author's keen intuitions had failed or fled from her. Nor when her work was done would she consent to alter or amend at the bidding of others; for the sake of no applause, of no success, would she change the fate of any of her characters as they had been fixed in the crucible of her genius. Even when her father exerted all his authority to secure another ending to the tale of "Villette," he could only, as we have seen, persuade his daughter to veil the catastrophe. The hero was doomed; and Charlotte, whatever might be her own inclination, could not save him from his fate. Books so true, so honest, so simple, so thorough as these, depend for their ultimate fate upon no transitions of fashion, no caprices of the public taste. They will hold their own as the slow-born fruits of a great genius, long after the productions of a score of facile pens now able to secure the world's attention have been utterly forgotten. The daring and passion of "Jane Eyre," the broad human sympathies, sparkling humour, and graphic portraiture of "Shirley," and the steady, patient, unsurpassed concentration of power which distinguishes "Villette," can hardly cease to command admiration whilst the literature of this century is remembered and studied.

But when we turn from the author to the woman, from the written pages to the writer, and when, forgetting the features and fortunes of those who appear in the romances of "Currer Bell," we recall that touching story which will for ever be associated with

Haworth Parsonage and with the great family of the Brontës, we see that the artist is greater than her works, that the woman is nobler and purer than the writer, and that by her life, even more than by her labours, the author of "Jane Eyre" must always teach us those lessons of courage, self-sacrifice, and patient endurance of which our poor humanity stands in such pressing and constant need.

THE END.

FOOTNOTES

[1] "Charles Kingsley: his Letters and Memories of his Life," vol. ii. p. 24.
[2] Harper's *New Monthly Magazine*, February, 1866.

www.ingramcontent.com/pod-product-compliance
Lightning Source LLC
Chambersburg PA
CBHW030108170426
43198CB00009B/542